SPOT DRILLS
Low Intermediate

RAYNER W. MARKLEY
WILLARD D. SHEELER

LOW
INTERMEDIATE

SPOT DRILLS

ILLUSTRATED
GRAMMAR
EXERCISES

OXFORD UNIVERSITY PRESS
1983

Oxford University Press

200 Madison Avenue
New York, N.Y. 10016 USA

Walton Street
Oxford OX2 6DP England

OXFORD is a trademark of Oxford University Press.

Library of Congress Cataloging in Publication Data

Markley, Rayner.
　　Spot drills.

　　Contents: 1. Elementary.
　　1. English language—Text-books for foreign speakers.
2. English language—Grammar—1950- .
I. Sheeler, Willard De Mont, 1915- . II. Title.
PE1128.M337　1983　　428.2'4　　83-2264
ISBN 0-19-434125-9

Copyright © 1983 by Oxford University Press, Inc.

First published 1983

First impression 1983

All rights reserved. No part of this publication may be reproduced, stored in a retrieval system, or transmitted, in any form or by any means, electronic, mechanical, photocopying, recording, or otherwise, without the prior permission of Oxford University Press.

This book is sold subject to the condition that it shall not, by way of trade or otherwise, be lent, resold, hired out, or otherwise circulated without the publisher's prior consent in any form of binding or cover other than that in which it is published and without a similar condition including this condition being imposed on the subsequent purchaser.

Illustrations by Dennis Kendrick.

Printed in the United States of America.

PREFACE

Spot Drills provides practice material on specific grammatical points for learners of English as a second language and is designed for use with any major textbook series or as self-study practice.

The 110 units of *Spot Drills: Low Intermediate* cover the grammatical structures and forms which are usually taught in elementary level courses. These one-page units are arranged in three sections: (1) Points concerning the verb phrase (verb inflection, tenses, auxiliaries, etc.); (2) Points concerning the noun phrase (noun inflection, determiners, pronouns, etc.); and (3) Types of sentences (objects, complements, types of questions, imperatives, etc.).

It is not intended or necessary to do the units in order. One can start anywhere and skip around as needed. This is facilitated by the page-by-page format and by the limited vocabulary and structure items used throughout the book. Only structures that have specific units on them are used anywhere in the book. There are, for example, no embedded clauses, passives, or present perfect verb phrases at this level. Furthermore, some structures are not used outside of the units devoted to them. Tag questions are only in the five units 95 through 99. Other examples of such restricted use include negative questions and *There* sentences. The irregular past forms of the 61 verbs presented in Units 23 through 26 (and listed in Appendix B) may be used throughout the book.

Vocabulary follows the major elementary textbooks in using the areas of nationality, language, food, clothing, and objects of the home, classroom, office, and shops. Some additional vocabulary, not commonly found at the elementary level, is used to make some exercises workable and more interesting. Whenever possible vocabulary words are alphabetized. Some of these words are pictured in the drills.

The Drills

"Drills" is a term used loosely; not only mechanical or fluency drills, but also exercises which require making a choice or creating sentences are found in this book. A progression in the different parts of a unit helps develop fluency in using the grammatical forms, building from simple word formation or substitution to sentence completion or the formation of entire sentences. A completed example is always given to get the drill started. There are three principle types of drills.

Substitution drills require a substitution and usually another change (such as a pronoun or an auxiliary) in the sentence (e.g., 46A). There are also so-called progressive substitutions, in which two different parts of the sentence are substituted (e.g., 71A). Some of these also require a change in the sentence. In the example sentence for a substitution drill the item or items to be replaced are underlined, and the item that changes (if any) is **boldfaced**.

Fill-in exercises require that a word (or group of words) be added to complete a sentence. It may be a function word (e.g., 52B) or a word chosen from a list (e.g., 45B) or from two words in parentheses (e.g., 43A).

Sentence formation exercises, as the name indicates, require that complete sentences be formed. Usually a model is given and other sentences are to be formed like it (e.g., 50B), sometimes in answer to a question (e.g., 54A). In some cases cued words are given in scrambled order (e.g., 43C); some are matching exercises (e.g., 47A). When two different sentences are to be formed, the cued words for each sentence are separated by double slashes // (e.g., 52A). Sentence completion exercises are similar to fill-ins or sentence formation except that the sentence is begun for the student (e.g., 47C, 64A).

Many drills have provision for two students to take part (e.g., 45C, 46C, 47B). In making a reply in these, and in any drill or exercise, only natural responses should be used. This means making any necessary pronoun substitution and shortening of predicates.

The use of integral pictures or tables in each unit is a feature of this exercise book that allows for considerable communication practice and creativity on the part of the student. Note that the student is not asked to give a grammatical analysis.

Supplementary Material
The supplementary material at the back of the book includes appendices of helpful grammatical tables, some teacher's notes, and an answer key. This section of teacher's notes has some ideas and suggestions for expanding the drills (that is, doing them again in a slightly different way) or cross-references to other pertinent drills or pictures. Since more than one page of practice will be needed for some grammatical points, teachers are encouraged to adapt other drills frequently. There are also notes in this section to clarify certain aspects of drills that may not be obvious. However, there is no general grammatical explanation in the book. It is expected that the teacher will provide whatever is needed before doing the drills. The examples at the beginning of each unit do focus on the purpose of the unit.

The drills can be used in a variety of language learning situations to supplement courses organized from widely different approaches. Whether coming to a new grammatical topic or spotting a need for extra practice, the teacher can quickly turn to the appropriate Spot Drill.

April 1983

R.W.M.
W.D.S.

CONTENTS

Section One VERB PHRASES

Present of *Be*	Present Continuous	Future
Past of *Be*	Past Tense	Auxiliary *Can*
Present Tense	Past Continuous	*Have* and *Want* + Infinitive

1. Present of *be*: Affirmative
2. Present of *be*: Affirmative Contractions
3. Present of *be*: Negative (*is/'s not*)
4. Present of *be*: Negative (*isn't*)
5. Present of *be*: Questions and Short Answers
6. Present of *be*: Question Word Questions
7. Past of *be*: Affirmative and Negative
8. Past of *be*: Questions and Short Answers
9. Present Tense: *-s* Form
10. Present Tense: Affirmative
11. Present Tense: Negative
12. Present Tense: Questions and Short Answers
13. Present Tense: Question Word Questions
14. Present Continuous: Affirmative
15. Present Continuous: Negative
16. Present Continuous: Questions and Short Answers
17. Present Continuous: Compared with Simple Present Tense
18. Present Continuous: Avoided by Certain Verbs
19. Present Continuous: Question Word Questions
20. Past Tense: Regular *-ed* Form
21. Past Tense: Affirmative and Negative
22. Past Tense: Questions and Short Answers
23. Past Tense: 13 Irregular Verb Forms
24. Past Tense: 15 Irregular Verb Forms
25. Past Tense: 16 Irregular Verb Forms
26. Past Tense: 17 Irregular Verb Forms
27. Past Tense: Summary of Regular and Irregular Verbs
28. Past Tense: Question Word Questions
29. Past Continuous: Affirmative and Negative

30. Past Continuous: Questions and Short Answers
31. Past Continuous Compared with Simple Past
32. Future *be going to*: Affirmative and Negative
33. Future *be going to*: Questions and Short Answers
34. Future *will*: Affirmative and Negative
35. Future *will*: Questions and Short Answers
36. Future: Question Word Questions
37. Future: Summary
38. Auxiliary *can*
39. Verbs *have* and *want* + Infinitive
40. Summary of Verb Forms
41. Summary of Negative Sentences
42. Summary of Yes/No Questions and Short Answers

Section Two   NOUN PHRASES

Nouns	Substitutes	Compound Noun Phrases
Articles	Pronouns	
Modifiers	Quantifiers	

43. Nouns: Uses of Nouns
44. Nouns: Regular Plural Forms
45. Nouns: Irregular Plural Forms
46. Nouns: Singular vs. Plural Nouns
47. Nouns: Countable vs. Noncountable Nouns
48. Nouns: Possessive Forms
49. Nouns: Summary of Forms
50. Article *a* vs. *an*
51. Article *the*: Uses of *the*
52. Article *a/an* vs. *the*
53. Modifiers and Substitutes: Possessive Nouns
54. Modifiers and Substitutes: Adjectives and Adjective + *one*
55. Modifiers and Substitutes: Ordinals

56. Modifiers and Substitutes: Demonstratives
57. Modifiers: *other*
58. Substitutes: *other (one)*
59. Personal Pronouns: Subject
60. Personal Pronouns: Object
61. Personal Pronouns: Possessive Modifiers
62. Personal Pronouns: Possessive
63. Personal Pronouns: Reflexive
64. Personal Pronouns: Summary
65. Quantifiers: *some, any*
66. Quantifiers: *some, any* vs. *a/an, one*
67. Quantifiers: *many, much*
68. Quantifiers: *many, much* vs. *a lot of*
69. Quantifiers: *a few, a little*
70. Quantifiers: *few, little, no, none*
71. Quantifiers: Before Other Modifiers
72. Quantifiers: *both, all, each, every*
73. Quantifiers: *half, quarter,* etc.
74. Summary of Articles and Other Modifiers
75. Summary of Pronouns and Other Substitutes
76. Compound Noun Phrases with *and*
77. Compound Noun Phrases with *or*

Section Three   TYPES OF SENTENCES

Types of Verbs and Complements	Negative Questions
There Sentences	Adverbials
Question Word Questions	Conjunctions *and, but,* and *or*
Tag Questions	

78. Sentences with *be* and Complement
79. Sentences with Linking Verb and Complement
80. Sentences with Verb and Direct Object

81. Sentences with No Direct Objects
82. Sentences with Indirect Objects
83. Sentences with *to* or *for* + Indirect Object
84. Sentences with *be* vs. *do* Verbs
85. *There* Sentences: Affirmative and Negative
86. *There* Sentences: Questions and Short Answers
87. Question Word Questions: *who* and *what* as Subject
88. Question Word Questions: *who* and *what* as Object
89. Question Word Questions: *which*
90. Question Word Questions: *whose*
91. Question Word Questions: *where*
92. Question Word Questions: *when*
93. Question Word Questions: *how many* and *how much*
94. Question Word Questions: Summary
95. Tag Questions with the Verb *be*
96. Tag Questions with Continuous Tenses
97. Tag Questions with the Auxiliary *do*
98. Tag Questions with *there* Sentences
99. Tag Questions: Summary
100. Negative Questions with the Verb *be*
101. Negative Questions with the Auxiliary *do*
102. Adverbials: Place
103. Adverbials: Time
104. Adverbials: Order of Place and Time
105. Adverbials: Frequency
106. Conjunction *and*
107. Conjunction *but*
108. Conjunction *but* in Short Clauses
109. Conjunction *and* vs. *but*
110. Conjunction *or*

Teacher's Notes   111

Answer Key   116

Appendices   129

SPOT DRILLS
Low Intermediate

SECTION ONE

1 Present of be: Affirmative

am   is   are

A. Form sentences like the model. Substitute the subject. Use **am, are,** or **is.**

<u>We</u> **are** warm.

Ex. She
She is warm.

1. You
2. I
3. It
4. They
5. He
6. She and I
7. Mrs. Jessup
8. Mr. and Mrs. Winter
9. The animals
10. This milk
11. Her hand
12. The children

B. Fill in the blanks with **am, are,** or **is.**

1. This room ___is___ small.
2. Those buildings _____ stores.
3. Ralph _____ a dentist.
4. They _____ on the floor.
5. I _____ in the class.
6. Ralph and you _____ late.
7. Swimming _____ my favorite sport.
8. The lamp and the vase _____ broken.
9. Mr. and Mrs. Watson _____ here.
10. I _____ a new student.
11. Mrs. Jessup, you _____ wonderful.
12. Your sister _____ outside.
13. The boss and I _____ forty years old.
14. His parents _____ in South America.
15. Mrs. Jones and her daughter _____ in Room 606.

C. Form sentences about the picture. Use a form of **be** and an adjective from the list.

angry   dirty   hot   hungry

1. (The milk)
   The milk is hot.
2. (The kittens)
3. (Their feet)
4. (Mrs. Winter)

2 Present of be: Affirmative Contractions

I'm	we're
you're	you're
he's, she's, it's	they're

A. Form sentences like the model. Substitute the subject pronoun or the complement of **be**. Use the correct contracted form of **be**. Do 1–13 in order.

<u>She's in this room.</u>

Ex. We
We're in this room.

1. He
2. on the phone
3. You
4. by the door
5. I
6. It
7. in the box
8. They
9. very nice
10. She
11. a pilot
12. I
13. ready now

B. Fill in the blanks with words in parentheses and a form of **be**. Use the contraction **'s** if possible (**the bat's** but **the class is**).

1. The <u>ball's</u> lost. (ball)
2. Your <u>watch is</u> on the desk. (watch)
3. An _____ a big animal. (elephant)
4. _____ the time? (What)
5. That _____ a good place. (college)
6. The _____ over. (class)
7. _____ that young man? (Who)
8. _____ Mr. Frantz? (Where)
9. This _____ rough. (ride)
10. Her _____ next to mine. (house)
11. The _____ beautiful. (garden)
12. _____ on the dining room table. (A vase)

C. Study the picture. Student 1: complete the question. Use **what** or **where**. Student 2: answer each question.

1. <u>Where's</u> Miss Jacobs?
   At her desk. (or) **She's at her desk.**
2. _____ in the vase?
3. _____ the scissors?
4. _____ the letters?
5. _____ on the table?
6. _____ on the file cabinet?

3 Present of be: Negative (is/'s not)

I **am** not.	I'**m** not.
You **are** not.	You'**re** not.
He **is** not.	He'**s** not.

A. Form sentences like the model. Substitute the subject pronoun or the complement of **be**. Use the correct contracted form of **be**. Do 1-12 in order.

<u>It'</u>s not <u>right</u>.

Ex. They
They're not right.

1. You
2. in the right place
3. It
4. We
5. She
6. a good swimmer
7. I
8. He
9. You
10. good swimmers
11. They
12. ready

B. Fill in the blanks with the correct full form of **be** and the word **not**.

1. The waiters <u>are not</u> in the kitchen.
2. The milk _____ in the refrigerator.
3. The car _____ in the garage.
4. The children _____ in their room.
5. The park _____ clean.
6. The air and water _____ the same temperature.
7. Our teacher _____ an American.
8. Mr. Kessler and I _____ accountants.
9. A whale _____ a fish.
10. Howard and Bill _____ engineers.
11. You and Mrs. Schetter _____ late.
12. Your glasses _____ on right.

C. Study the picture. Complete the sentences. Use **are** or **'s**. The first sentence will be negative.

1. The driver<u>'s not in the taxi.</u> <u>He's</u> in the diner.
2. One door_____. _____ shut.
3. The suitcases _____. _____ on the sidewalk.
4. The headlights _____. _____ on.
5. That lady _____. _____ the passenger.

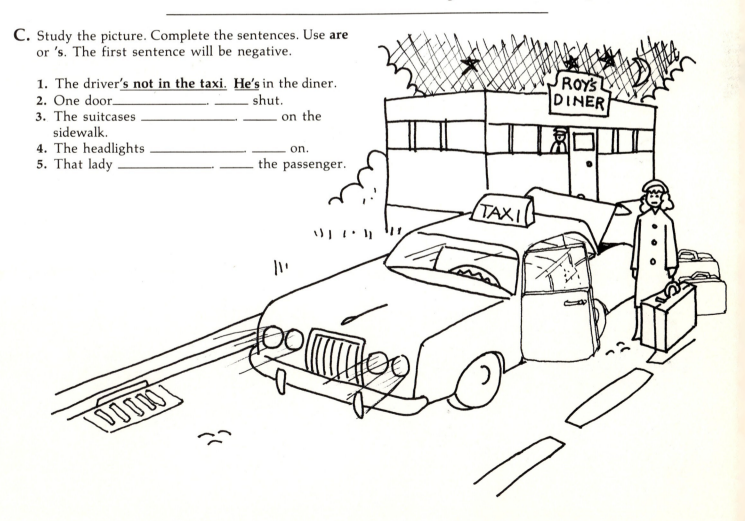

4 Present of be: Negative (isn't)

He/She/It	isn't
We/You/They	aren't

A. Form sentences like the model. Substitute the subject. Use the verb **isn't** or **aren't**.

The glass **isn't** full.

Ex. The cups
The cups aren't full.

1. The theater
2. The trash cans
3. My stomach
4. Her wallet
5. My suitcases
6. The airplane
7. The elevators
8. Many buses
9. Her calendar
10. The bag
11. His pockets
12. That bottle

B. Fill in the blanks with a pronoun and **isn't** or **aren't**.

1. Rocks are hard. **They aren't** soft.
2. Butter's yellow. _____ red.
3. Mr. Aoki's Japanese. _____ Chinese.
4. The cows are lost. _____ here.
5. The house is across the street. _____ on the corner.
6. Your shirts are at the cleaners. _____ in the closet.
7. That girl's a cafeteria worker. _____ a student.
8. Penguins are birds. _____ fish.
9. This ring's for Carol. _____ for you.
10. Those boxes are only half full. _____ ready.
11. The typewriter is over here. _____ electric.
12. The salt and pepper are in the kitchen. _____ on the table.

C. Form a negative and an affirmative sentence about each picture.

1. The dishes **aren't clean**. **They're dirty**. (clean, dirty)
2. The books _____ _____ . (closed, open)
3. The street _____ _____ . (quiet, noisy)
4. John _____ _____ (single, married)
5. The juice _____ _____ . (sweet, sour)
6. The turtle _____ _____ . (quick, slow)
7. The rabbit _____ _____ . (quick, slow)

THE RABBIT IS QUICK.
THE TURTLE IS SLOW.

5 Present of be: Questions and Short Answers

Is	she	a nurse?	Yes,	she	**is**.
Are	they	at home?	No,	they	**aren't**.
Are	you	ready?	No,	I'm	**not**.

A. Student 1: ask questions like the model. Student 2: give short **yes** or **no** answers. Do 1–12 in order.

Is he a mechanic?

Ex. Mary
Is Mary a mechanic? Yes, she is.

1. in the garage
2. the tools
3. Bill
4. hungry
5. they
6. tired
7. you (plural)
8. the teacher
9. your friend
10. in the hospital
11. on the second floor
12. all right

B. Student 1: read the sentence. Then ask a yes/no question. Student 2: give a short answer like the example.

Ex. Bill's tired. (Mary//Yes)
Is Mary tired? Yes, she is.

1. I'm afraid. (you//No)
2. That clock's wrong. (your watch//No)
3. Her hair's brown. (her eyes //Yes)
4. The car's in the garage. (the tools//Yes)
5. The potatoes are in the oven. (the cookies//No)
6. Mary's at the hospital. (Bill//Yes)
7. I'm out of white paper. (the typist//No)
8. Miss Warner's here. (Mr. and Mrs. Young//Yes)
9. You're in the front row. (I//No)
10. These are cheese sandwiches. (That//Yes)

C. Student 1: ask questions about each picture. Use words from the list. Student 2: give a short **yes** or **no** answer.

happy   heavy   hungry   light
lively   thirsty   tired   unhappy

1. **Is the East team happy? Yes, it is.**
   (or) **Are the East players unhappy? No, they aren't.**

6 Present of be: Question Word Questions

$$
\begin{array}{l}
\text{Who} \\
\text{What}
\end{array}\Big\} \text{ is a librarian?}
$$

$$
\begin{array}{l}
\text{Where} \\
\text{When}
\end{array}\Big\} \text{ are the meetings?}
$$

A. Fill in the blanks with a question word and **is** or **are**.

1. **Where's** Marie's house? On 44th Street.
2. _____ the games? On the weekends.
3. _____ the captain? Simpson is.
4. _____ the winners? Stella and Mike.
5. _____ your boots? In the closet.
6. _____ the next train? Pretty soon.
7. _____ those things? Radios.
8. _____ that young man? My big brother.
9. _____ their names? Smith and Brown.
10. _____ Joyce? At the library.

B. Student 1: read the sentence. Student 2: ask a question about the words in parentheses. Use a question word. Student 1: then choose an answer from the list.

A Ford.	In the summer.	Today.
The vegetables.	Fish.	Terry Jones.
His sister.	On Q Street.	

Ex. Annette Jones is my brother's wife. (Julia Johnson)
Who's Julia Johnson? His sister.

1. The sales meeting's next Tuesday. (the election of officers)
2. Penguins are birds. (sharks)
3. Steve's car is a Volkswagen. (Martha's car)
4. Brian's birthday is in February. (his brothers' birthdays)
5. The chicken is in the oven. (the refrigerator)
6. The library's on Grand Avenue. (the railroad station)
7. Winters is the vice-president. (the president)

C. Study the pictures. Student 1: ask questions with **what's, where's**, or **where are**. Student 2: answer each question.

1. **What's on the table? A birthday cake.**
   (or) **Where's the birthday cake? On the table.**

7 Past of be: Affirmative and Negative

was	were
wasn't	weren't

A. Form sentences like the model. Substitute the subject. Use **was** or **were**.

The dishes **were** in the kitchen.

Ex. She
She was in the kitchen.

1. Some glasses
2. We
3. The napkins
4. It
5. The butter
6. I
7. Al and Vic
8. He
9. The vegetables
10. The cookbook
11. They
12. The rice

B. Form a negative and an affirmative sentence like the example.

Ex. She/fat//thin
She wasn't fat. She was thin.

1. We/interested//bored
2. He/young//old
3. They/in New York//in Miami
4. You/in your house//in a restaurant
5. I/vice-president//president
6. His grandfather/from Belgium//from Holland
7. Miss Wade/the teacher//a student
8. The school/in the suburbs//downtown
9. He and I/good swimmers//just beginners
10. Helen/married//single
11. Mr. Greer/in the office//at lunch

C. Form negative and affirmative sentences about the picture. Use the past forms of **be**.

1. The cat ____.
   The cat wasn't inside.
   The cat was outside.
2. The windows ____.
3. The key ____.
4. Mrs. Kinkaid ____.
5. The door ____.
6. The piano ____.

8 Past of be: Questions and Short Answers

| **Was** | he | at home? | Yes, | he | **was.** |
| **Were** | they | students? | No, | they | **weren't.** |

A. Student 1: ask questions like the example. Use **was** or **were**. Student 2: give a short **yes** or **no** answer.

Ex. they/in the garage
  Were they in the garage? Yes, they were.

1. she/the receptionist
2. we/in the right building
3. I/right
4. you/ready for the trip
5. it/by the door
6. the letters/important
7. the Critchfields/at home
8. your friends/angry
9. Jean/a winner
10. Mr. Jamison/on that bus
11. you and your husband/downtown

B. Student 1: ask questions about subjects 1–12. Use **was** or **were** and a complement from the list a–l. Student 2: give a short answer.

1. the chair//Yes
2. the child//No
3. the cups//Yes
4. the doors//No
5. the front//Yes
6. the game//No
7. the islands//Yes
8. January//No
9. your office//Yes
10. the ropes//No
11. the toys//Yes
12. you and Al//No

a) exciting
b) like the back
c) lonesome
d) near the coast
e) on sale
f) above the classroom
g) shut
h) strong
i) together
j) a warm month
k) with the saucers
l) for little children

1. **Was the chair on sale? Yes, it was.**

C. Student 1: ask yes/no questions about each picture. Student 2: give short **yes** or **no** answers.

1. (Al)
   Was Al a good boy? No, he wasn't.
2. (many people)
3. (the apples)
4. (the brakes)

Present Tense: -s Form

mean	**means**	/z/*
make	**makes**	/s/
miss	**misses**	/ɪz/

A. Form the **-s** form of these verbs. Put the **-s** form under its correct pronunciation.

		/z/	/s/	/ɪz/
1. dig	11. put	_____	_____	_____
2. feel	12. reach	_____	_____	_____
3. give	13. ring	_____	_____	_____
4. hear	14. rob	_____	_____	_____
5. judge	15. run	_____	_____	_____
6. know	16. seem	_____	_____	_____
7. laugh	17. stop			
8. look	18. try			
9. need	19. wish			
10. pass				

B. Fill in the blanks with the **-s** form of a verb from the list. Give the sound of the ending: /z/, /s/, or /ɪz/.

| ask | charge | fix | hold | march | serve | turn |
| burn | dance | help | last | park | sound | want |

1. That restaurant **serves** /z/ good food.
2. She _____ her mother in the kitchen.
3. He _____ broken watches.
4. My sister _____ in parades.
5. Dry wood _____ fast.
6. The bottle _____ one quart.
7. The teacher _____ hard questions.
8. He always _____ his car there.
9. Stanley _____ a new job.
10. This road _____ to the right.
11. A box of matches _____ four months.
12. The store _____ $3.00 for gift wrapping.
13. His voice _____ bad today.
14. Marion _____ very well at parties.

*The symbols within / / represent **sounds**, not spelling.

10 Present Tense: Affirmative

> I/We/You/They **run.**
> He/She/It **runs.**

A. Form sentences like the model. Substitute the subject. Use the plain form or the -s form of the verb.

He always **leaves** at one o'clock.

Ex. I
I always leave at one o'clock.

1. The bus
2. We
3. Mr. Toby
4. You
5. The president
6. They
7. It
8. She and I
9. Our class
10. Her children
11. The mail
12. That flight

B. Fill in the blanks with the -s form or plain form of a verb on the list.

| ask | cross | earn | get | speak | taste |
| come | drink | fall | sit | take | use |

1. Seattle __gets__ a lot of rain.
2. Rain _____ ten months of the year.
3. Many storms _____ from the east.
4. Our car _____ a lot of gas.
5. Your cookies _____ very good.
6. Dad _____ in that chair.
7. We always _____ for chopsticks at the restaurant.
8. The Kellys _____ $30,000 a year.
9. My brother _____ Russian quite well.
10. Jerry _____ his lunch to work every day.
11. I _____ a glass of milk every morning.
12. This street _____ Main Street up there.

C. Study the pictures. Form sentences about Carol's daily routine.

1. Carol gets up at 7:00 every morning.

11 Present Tense: Negative

> I/We/You/They **don't** run.
> He/She/It **doesn't** run.

A. Form sentences like the model. Substitute the subject or the verb. Use **don't** or **doesn't**. Do 1–12 in order.

The sky **doesn't** look bad.

Ex. Those curtains
Those curtains don't look bad.

1. Mary
2. You
3. sound
4. This radio
5. They
6. feel
7. I
8. His new shoes
9. smell
10. This milk
11. taste
12. The meat

B. Fill in the blanks with **doesn't** or **don't** and a verb in the parentheses.

1. Fish <u>don't fly</u>. (fly, swim)
2. This pencil _____ well. (read, write)
3. Her sisters _____ here. (keep, live)
4. The sun _____ in the east. (fall, set)
5. My ears _____ cold. (feel, smell)
6. It _____ every day in the summer. (rain, snow)
7. Shoes _____ $300. (cost, last)
8. The paper _____ a hole in it. (find, have)
9. Banks _____ at seven o'clock. (begin, open)
10. The next lesson _____ on page 32. (begin, open)
11. My teachers _____ a cassette player. (use, write)
12. A quarter _____ 33 cents. (equal, add)

C. Form a negative sentence about each picture. Use verbs from the list.

drive   have   swim   understand

1. **The boy doesn't swim well.**

12 Present Tense: Questions and Short Answers

Does	it	**look**	good?	Yes,	it	**does.**
Do	they	**look**	good?	No,	they	**don't.**

A. Student 1: complete the questions like the example. Use a verb from the list. Student 2: complete the answers.

eat   have   hurt   know   like   live   look   make   need   seem   stop   use

Ex. **Does** Miyoko **know** English well?   Yes, **she does.**

1. _____ your fingers _____?   No, _____.
2. _____ this lesson _____ easy?   No, _____.
3. _____ the crosstown bus _____ here?   Yes, _____.
4. _____ the Olsons _____ a new house?   Yes, _____.
5. _____ your teacher _____ his job?   Yes, _____.
6. _____ ten years _____ like a century?   No, _____.
7. _____ you _____ a soft toothbrush?   Yes, _____.
8. _____ I _____ another appointment?   No, _____.
9. _____ Sally _____ a lot of candy?   Yes, _____.
10. _____ it _____ like rain?   No, _____.
11. _____ Akiko and her family _____ in the U.S.? No, _____.

B. Student 1: read the question. Student 2: answer the question. Then substitute the words in parentheses in the correct place in the question. Make any other necessary changes. Student 1: give a short **yes** or **no** answer.

Ex. Do your friends speak English? (Enrico)
Yes, they do. Does Enrico speak English? **No, he doesn't.**

1. Does it snow here during the winter? (rain)
2. Do you cook with butter? (Miss Long)
3. Do they drink coffee? (you—plural)
4. Does your sister feel all right? (your parents)
5. Do I have your address? (telephone number)
6. Do you understand Chinese? (your friend)
7. Do the bananas taste good? (the dessert)
8. Does the train leave on time? (the buses)
9. Do you wear eyeglasses? (a hat)
10. Does the store open at 9:00? (the stores)
11. Does your family own a house? (the Wilsons)

C. Student 1: ask yes/no questions about the airline schedule. Use **do** or **does**. Student 2: give short **yes** or **no** answers.

Ex. Does Flight 404 leave at 10:00? Yes, it does. (or) Does Flight 612 leave from Gate 4? No, it doesn't.

AIRLINE SCHEDULE Departures			
FLIGHT	DESTINATION	DEPART	GATE
404	Boston	10:00 a.m.	4
612	Chicago	11:15 a.m.	6
492	Honolulu	12:00 p.m.	8
526	St. Louis	12:30 p.m.	9
900	Tokyo	5:00 p.m.	1

13 Present Tense: Question Word Questions

Who
What } does Pat like?

Where
When } do you eat?

A. Fill in the blanks with a question word and **does** or **do**.

1. **When does** that bus leave? — At 10:00 a.m.
2. _____ she teach? — At Baxter School.
3. _____ you eat for lunch? — A bowl of soup.
4. _____ the baby wake up? — At 3:00 a.m.
5. _____ the Wilsons live? — In Rockdale.
6. _____ I need for the test? — Paper and pencils.
7. _____ John listen to? — His father.
8. _____ the taxis stop? — At the next corner.
9. _____ Mr. Simms teach? — American history.
10. _____ you have lunch with? — Miriam Faber.

B. Student 1: read the sentence. Student 2: ask a question word question about the subject in parentheses. Student 1: then choose a short answer from the list.

After supper.   In St. Louis.   The same time.
Eggs.   On the rug.   Walter.
The news.   Stand.

Ex. George lives in New Orleans. (Phil)
Where does Phil live? In St. Louis.

1. Bill eats cereal for breakfast. (his wife)
2. My dog sleeps on the sofa. (your cat)
3. Julie likes Jack. (Mary)
4. "Pass away" means "die." ("get up")
5. Ken watches sports on TV. (Harold)
6. High school classes begin in September. (university classes)
7. Henry studies early in the morning. (his roommate)

C. Student 1: ask a question word question about each picture. Use a verb from the list. Student 2: answer the questions.

begin   keep   like   study
cost   leave   smell   work

1. **When does the next movie begin? At 7:30 p.m.**

14 Present Continuous: Affirmative

I	**am/'m working**	hard.
They	**are/'re planning**	a report.
She	**is/'s riding**	a bicycle.

A. Form sentences like the model. Substitute the subject. Use **am**, **are**, or **is**.

You **are** getting cold.

Ex. She
She is getting cold.

1. They
2. It
3. We
4. He
5. I
6. Miss Fisher
7. The potatoes
8. Your dinner
9. This room
10. Shirley and I
11. The children
12. My fingers

B. Fill in the blanks with a verb from the list. Use the present continuous.

| buy | go | learn | rain | sleep | spend |
| get | grow | make | run | speak | work |

1. It **'s raining** in St. Louis.
2. Jim _____ on the sofa.
3. Mrs. White _____ a new coat.
4. The car _____ smoothly.
5. Her tomatoes and corn _____ very well.
6. She _____ a sweater for you.
7. I _____ for an automobile company.
8. We _____ our money fast.
9. Mr. Stone and I _____ French.
10. We _____ to speak English.
11. The weather _____ warm.
12. I _____ to the library.

C. Form a sentence about each picture. Use the present continuous form of verbs from the list.

| fill | watch | arrive | wash |
| pack | cry | return | kiss |

1. The woman is filling the glasses.

15 Present Continuous: Negative

She   is/'s not/isn't working   on a report.
They   are/'re not/aren't working   downtown.
I   am/'m not working   hard.

A. Form a sentence like the model. Substitute the subject. Use **aren't, isn't,** or **am not.**

He **isn't** eating rice.

Ex. We
We aren't eating rice.

1. She
2. You
3. I
4. They
5. Earl
6. Earl and I
7. The baby
8. The animals
9. Those guests
10. The American
11. The waiter
12. The children

B. Read each sentence. Then form a negative sentence. Use the object or complement in parentheses.

Ex. He's changing his shirt. (his socks)
He isn't changing his socks.

1. We're drinking water. (milk)
2. It's getting cold. (warm)
3. They're sending food. (medicine)
4. She's washing the dishes. (the clothes)
5. I'm writing a letter. (a book)
6. The nurse is moving the lamp. (the bed)
7. He's buying a pair of pants. (a suit)
8. That patient is calling the nurse. (the doctor)
9. Mr. Robb is helping his sister. (his brother)
10. He and I are speaking French. (German)
11. I'm making bread. (a cake)

C. Form an affirmative sentence about each picture. Then use the verb in parentheses and form a negative sentence.

1. (drive)
   He's riding a bike.
   He isn't driving a car.
2. (build)
3. (read)
4. (run)

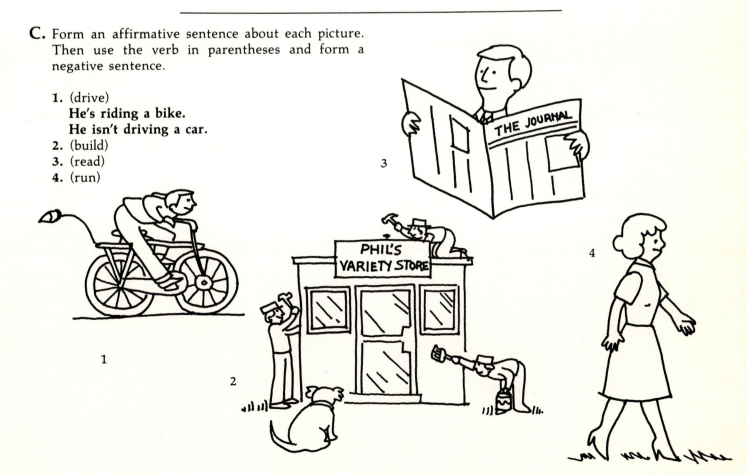

16 Present Continuous: Questions and Short Answers

Is	he	**working**	today?	Yes,	he	**is.**
Are	they	**waiting**?		No,	they	**aren't.**
Are	you	**watching**	us?	No,	I'm	**not.**

A. Student 1: ask a question like the model. Use the correct form of **be**. Student 2: give a short **yes** answer. Do 1-12 in order.

    Is he coming? Yes, he is.

Ex. they
    Are they coming? Yes, they are.

1. go
2. we
3. win
4. I
5. lose
6. you
7. come
8. the bus
9. leave
10. Mr. and Mrs. Wilson
11. your daughter
12. call

B. Student 1: fill in the blanks with the present continuous verb phrase. Use a verb from the list. Student 2: give a short answer.

chew cool correct get have make practice read stand study wash wear

1. __Is__ Miss Lewis **wearing** her coat?   Yes, __she is__ .
2. _____ the teacher _____ the mistakes?   No. _____.
3. _____ the kids _____ their hands?   Yes, _____.
4. _____ your soup _____ off fast?   No, _____.
5. _____ the neighbors _____ a party?   Yes, _____.
6. _____ Randy _____ the piano?   No, _____.
7. _____ I _____ in the right place?   Yes, _____.
8. _____ the trucks _____ a lot of noise?   No, _____.
9. _____ the sky _____ cloudy?   Yes, _____.
10. _____ you _____ your food well?   No, _____.
11. _____ your brother and sister _____ in Chicago?   Yes, _____.
12. _____ he _____ the business news?   No, _____.

C. Student 1: form a yes/no question about each picture. Use the verbs in the present continuous. Student 2: give a short **yes** or **no** answer.

1. (change)
   Is he changing a light bulb?
   Yes, he is.
2. (skate)
3. (eat)
4. (watch)

17 Present Continuous: Compared with Simple Present Tense

I **study** English every day.
I**'m studying** English now.

A. Form sentences like the model. Substitute the verb or the time expression. Change the tense when necessary. Do 1–12 in order.

   She exercises every day.

Ex. now
   She's exercising now.

1. play
2. every morning
3. practice
4. now
5. swim
6. every week
7. study
8. today
9. teach
10. on Fridays
11. work
12. this week

B. Student 1: ask a yes/no question like the example. Use the present tense and the word **often**. Student 2: give a short **yes** answer. Then form negative and affirmative sentences with the present continuous.

Ex. play tennis//play chess
   **Does he play tennis often? Yes, he does
   But he isn't playing tennis now. He's playing chess.**

1. speak Spanish//speak English
2. shop at Capwell's//shop at Murray's
3. drink coffee//drink tea
4. wash the car//wash the dog
5. listen to Russian music//listen to Spanish music
6. use black ink//use blue ink
7. watch TV//read a book
8. wear jeans//wear a suit
9. sit next to Darlene//sit next to Diane
10. save money//buy a motorcycle

C. Study the pictures. Answer each question with two sentences. Use one of the verbs in the simple present tense and the other verb in the present continuous.

1. What's Charles doing? call//read
   **He's reading the phone bill.
   He calls Walnut Creek often.**
2. What's Gordon doing? drive//paint
3. What does Rochelle do? cut//keep
4. What does Victor do? play//wait

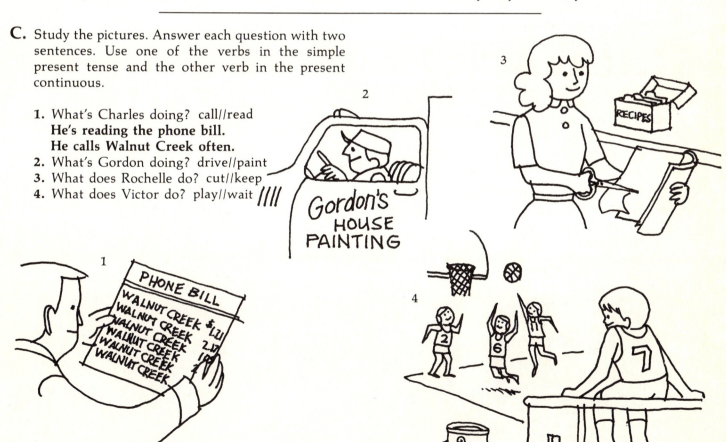

18 Present Continuous: Avoided by Certain Verbs

They **have** a big dog.
His food **costs** a lot of money.

A. Form sentences like the model. Substitute the verb. Use the present continuous if possible. Otherwise use the simple present tense.

    I am watching that bird now.

Ex. see
   I see that bird now.

1. look at
2. hear
3. listen to
4. like
5. call
6. want
7. buy
8. own
9. feed
10. remember
11. think about
12. know

B. Fill in the blanks with a verb in parentheses. Use the simple present or the present continuous.

1. She's **ordering** chicken. She **prefers** chicken. (order, prefer)
2. She _____ 125 pounds now. She _____ weigh. (lose, weigh)
3. We _____ ninety dollars for this. That _____ a day's pay. (equal, spend)
4. We _____ English. We _____ a lot of words already. (know, learn)
5. Jane _____ a dress. It _____ her very well. (fit, try on)
6. Look at Juan! He _____ English to Bill. He _____ it very well, too. (speak, understand)
7. I _____ a cake in the oven. It _____ good. Who _____ it? (bake, smell)
8. She _____ in the window now. She _____ her key on the table. (look, see)
9. I _____ another basket. This one _____ about sixty oranges. (hold, fill)
10. Ellen _____ your bike. She _____ to the corner and back. (have, ride)

C. Form two sentences about each picture. Use one verb in the simple present tense and the other verb in the present continuous.

   buy   look   want
   cost   look up
   laugh mean

1. **She's laughing. She looks happy.**

19 Present Continuous: Question Word Questions

Who
What } is Pat taking?

Where
When } are they going?

A. Read each sentence. Then form a question word question.

Ex. Jerry's going to Japan. (When)
When's he going?

1. Sharon is studying music. (Where)
2. Our neighbors are leaving for their vacation. (When)
3. Bob's inviting some people for dinner. (Who)
4. Tom's cooking tonight. (What)
5. Mrs. Follette's buying some clothes. (What)
6. The children are swimming. (Where)
7. George and Edith are coming to the meeting. (When)
8. Tom and Nancy are playing. (What)
9. Jane Nelson is calling a friend. (Who)

B. Student 1: read the sentence. Student 2: ask a question about the underlined words. Student 1: then give a short answer.

Ex. He's not going to Union today.
When is he going? On Friday.

1. I'm not watching the soccer game on TV.
2. Susan isn't crying about her clothes.
3. Jane isn't taking Stanley to the pool.
4. We aren't going to the library.
5. Alice isn't drinking tea.
6. Jean and I aren't speaking French.
7. The Smiths aren't eating in the cafeteria tonight.
8. I'm not making a birdhouse.
9. Mr. Brady's not going to Singapore on this trip.
10. I'm not going to the baseball game tonight.
11. Laura isn't practicing the piano.

C. Student 1: ask a question about each picture. Use the present continuous tense of a verb from the list. Student 2: give a short answer.

carry   have   lose   move

1. **Where are the Johnsons moving?**
   (To) Washington.

20 Past Tense: Regular -ed Form

call	**called**	/d/*
work	**worked**	/t/
wait	**waited**	/ɪd/

A. Form the -ed form of these verbs. Put the -ed form under its correct pronunciation.

		/ɪd/	/t/	/d/
1. add	8. pick	added		buzzed
2. buzz	9. play			
3. follow	10. point			
4. laugh	11. reach			
5. need	12. report			
6. open	13. seem			
7. pass	14. wish			

B. Form the -ed form of these verbs. Put the -ed form in column A, B, or C according to the spelling change.

		A. Last letter is doubled.	B. Last letter e is dropped.	C. Last letter y becomes i.
1. bake	7. like	batted	baked	carried
2. bat	8. move			
3. beg	9. plan			
4. carry	10. reply			
5. drop	11. study			
6. dry	12. tie			

C. Put the -ed form of one of the verbs in the list under each picture.

arrive, borrow, cry, fill, kiss, pack, wash, watch

1. filled 2. _____ 3. _____ 4. _____
5. _____ 6. _____ 7. _____ 8. _____

*The symbols within // represent **sounds**, not spelling.

21 Past Tense: Affirmative and Negative

| Jack | **wanted** | ice cream. |
| Mary | **didn't/did not want** | sugar in her tea. |

A. Read each sentence. Then form a negative sentence like the examples.

Ex. A. Bill studied English last night. (history)
He didn't study history.
Ex. B. Joe carried a suitcase. (Allan)
Allan didn't carry a suitcase.

1. It rained yesterday. (snow)
2. The dentist pulled one tooth. (two)
3. Henry borrowed $40. ($140)
4. She paid the carpenter. (the dentist)
5. We invited the Taylors. (the Johnsons)
6. I mailed Mrs. Long's package. (Mrs. Short's letter)
7. She washed the front windows. (the back ones)
8. We visited Paris. (London)
9. The corn tasted sweet. (bad)
10. He worked on Saturday. (on Sunday)
11. Mr. Wren phoned in the afternoon. (in the morning)
12. The speaker talked about money. (about love)
13. Jerry saved $200. (His sister)
14. Sue remembered the road. (I)
15. She passed the traffic light. (stop at)
16. He cried about it. (laugh)

B. Study the pictures. Form negative and affirmative sentences like the example.

1. **Bill didn't paint the house. He painted the garage.**

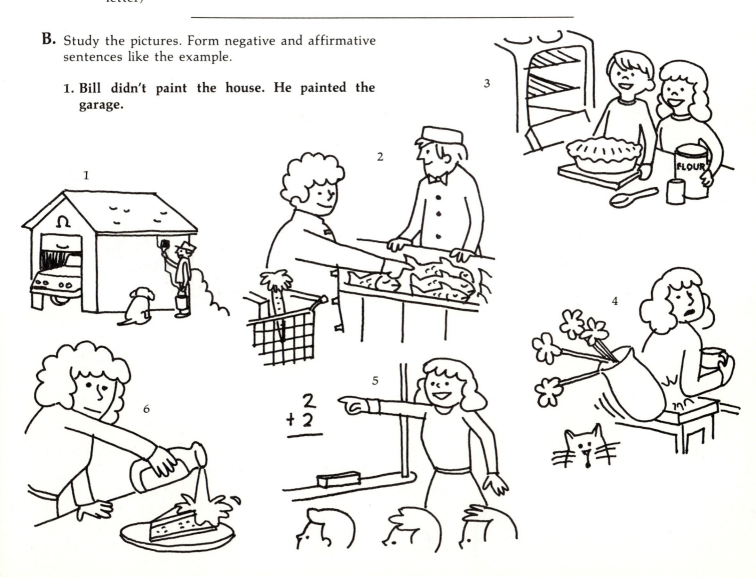

22 Past Tense: Questions and Short Answers

| Did | he | walk | here? | Yes, | he | did. |
| Did | you | cook | dinner? | No, | I | didn't. |

A. Form sentences like the model. Substitute the subject or the verb and complement. Do 1-12 in order.

   Did you fix the lamp?

   Ex. work hard
   Did you work hard?

   1. she
   2. lock the door
   3. return the book
   4. he
   5. use a red pen
   6. call Mr. Birch
   7. Andrea
   8. park on the street
   9. walk outside
   10. the Rowes
   11. watch TV
   12. you

B. Answer the questions with short **yes** or **no** answers.

   1. Did I pass the test? (Yes)
      Yes, you did.
   2. Did I get the highest mark? (No)
   3. Did John cross the street there? (Yes)
   4. Did his mother turn off the light? (No)
   5. Did the balloons belong to him? (Yes)
   6. Did you answer the phone? (No)
   7. Did the artist use paper? (Yes)
   8. Did the room seem small? (No)
   9. Did the plane arrive on time? (Yes)
   10. Did Margaret type the letter? (No)
   11. Did Joseph marry a waitress? (Yes)
   12. Did Suzie wash the truck? (No)

C. Study the pictures. Then form a short answer or a yes/no question.

   1. Did the mailman fall? **Yes, he did.**
      (drop) **Did he drop his letters?** No, he didn't.
   2. Did Valerie play tennis? _____.
      (break) _____ ? No, she didn't.
   3. Did Steve finish his milk? _____.
      (leave) _____ ? No, he didn't.
   4. Did the coffee taste good? _____.
      (cost) _____ ? Yes, it did.
   5. Did the Smiths go by car? _____.
      (wear) _____ ? No, they didn't.

23 Past Tense: 13 Irregular Verb Forms

cut **cut**
sell **sold**

A. Student 1: form a yes/no question like the example. Use the past tense of the verb. Student 2: answer **No, but** and a full sentence.

Ex. cut/arm//finger
Did you cut your arm? No, but I cut my finger.

1. sell/car//bike
2. hear/Billie//Susie
3. hurt/leg//foot
4. make/table//desk
5. shut/door//window
6. hit/head//arm
7. tell/John//Henry
8. do/housework//errands

B. Answer the questions like the example. Use full sentences.

Ex. What did Mrs. Harder cut? (her son's hair)
She cut her son's hair.

1. What did you hear? (a loud noise)
2. What did Paul shut? (the upstairs window)
3. What did Mary have at lunch? (a big glass of orange juice)
4. What did your brother sell? (his old TV)
5. Who did Fred tell? (Annabelle)
6. What did Ted do after dinner? (his math homework)
7. What did their house cost? (fifty thousand dollars)
8. What did Mrs. Wilson's car hit? (a small tree)
9. What did his wife say? (yes)
10. What did Tom do after dinner? (the dinner dishes)
11. What did Tommy put in the closet? (his lamp)
12. What did Phil's car cost? (two hundred dollars)
13. What did the teacher shut? (her book)

C. Form a sentence about each picture. Use the past tense.

hurt   make   put out   sell

1. **Mary hurt her head.**

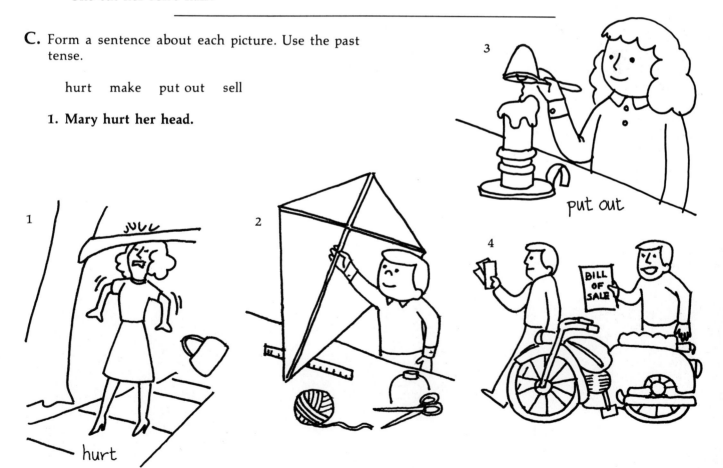

24 Past Tense: 15 Irregular Verb Forms

buy **bought**
lose **lost**

A. Fill in the blanks with the past form of a verb on the list.

bring	catch	leave	mean	spend
build	feel	lend	send	teach
buy	go	lose	sleep	think

1. She __went__ to a party last night.
2. I _____ eight hours last night.
3. He _____ her flowers yesterday.
4. He _____ his wallet on his trip.
5. He _____ about his girlfriend every day.
6. I _____ tired this morning.
7. She _____ the office early last Friday.
8. She _____ the four o'clock train.
9. He _____ a garage last summer.
10. I _____ my lunch to work today.
11. She _____ her children French on the weekends.
12. Helen _____ a newspaper at the drugstore.
13. They _____ me $500 for the trip.
14. They _____ $499 on the trip.
15. I said "I'm sorry" but I _____ "Thank you."

B. Student 1: ask a yes/no question like the examples. Use **you** as the subject. Student 2: answer with a negative and then an affirmative statement.

Ex. A. buy a new bike//old one
Did you buy a new bike?
No, I didn't buy a new one. I bought an old one.

Ex. B. go to Rome last summer//Paris
Did you go to Rome last summer?
No, I didn't go to Rome. I went to Paris.

1. lose your ring//my watch
2. leave the office at 6:00//5:00
3. build a model car//model airplane
4. spend $50//$30
5. teach Spanish//French
6. bring a salad//dessert
7. catch the 7:00 bus//the 8:00 bus
8. go to a movie yesterday afternoon//home

C. Study the pictures. Then fill in the blanks with the past form of the verbs in parentheses.

1. Helen __felt__ bad this morning. She __slept__ badly last night. (sleep, feel)
2. I _____ "Good-bye," but I _____ "Thank you." (say, mean)
3. Mrs. Horn _____ a new dress. She _____ $80 for it. (buy, spend)
4. Jim _____ the house at 6:00 and _____ the 6:30 train. (catch, leave)

25 Past Tense: 16 Irregular Verb Forms

take	**took**
begin	**began**

A. Student 1: ask a yes/no question. Use **Gary** as subject. Student 2: answer **no** in a full sentence.

Ex. forget his watch//his belt
 Did Gary forget his watch?
 No, he forgot his belt.

1. take/a bus//a taxi
2. speak/Italian//French
3. read/the newspaper//a magazine
4. win/$500//$100
5. meet/Tom//his brother
6. drink/coffee//tea
7. find/money//some papers
8. sing/in German//in Russian
9. get/a new car//an old car

B. Read the story. Then answer the questions. Use complete sentences.

John worked hard all week. Friday he got home late. His roommate was already home and opened the door for him.

"Oh, you look tired, John," he said. "Sit down and I'll fix you a sandwich.

"Thanks, George," John said. "I am tired. I think I'll eat and go to bed."

John ate, put on his red pajamas, and went to bed. George went out to the movies. John began to read a book. He read two pages and went to sleep.

At 10:00 p.m. the doorbell rang. Someone had the wrong apartment. John went back to bed. At 2:00 a.m. the telephone woke him up. "Happy Birthday," the caller sang. "Wrong number," John told him and tried to go to sleep again. At 6:00 a.m. the alarm clock woke him up.

"Well," John said to himself. "I don't think I slept at all, but I can't sleep now." He went out to the kitchen and George was there.

"My," George said. "You look fine this morning. There's nothing like a good night's sleep!"

1. When did John get home?
2. Who met him at the door?
3. Who gave John some food?
4. What did he eat and drink?
5. What did he wear to bed?
6. Where did George go?
7. John went to bed. Did he go right to sleep?
8. What woke him up? What time was this?
9. What woke John up in the middle of the night?
10. What did the person on the telephone do?
11. What time was this?
12. What happened early the next morning?
13. Did John go back to sleep?
14. Do you think he felt fine in the morning?

26 Past Tense: 17 Irregular Verb Forms

sit	**sat**
drive	**drove**

A. Fill in the blanks with the past form of a verb from the list.

draw	grow	lie	see	understand
fall	hold	ride	sit	
fly	know	run	stand	

1. He ___sat___ on a big chair.
2. She _____ a picture of a horse.
3. Try these tomatoes. I _____ them in my garden.
4. We spoke English. I _____ every word.
5. I was tired. I _____ down for an hour.
6. I liked our office manager. She _____ the office fairly.
7. My feet hurt tonight. I _____ for six hours today.
8. We _____ to London and Paris. Then we took the boat home.
9. It was an easy exam. I _____ all the answers.
10. Johnny _____ from the apple tree. Now he's in the hospital.
11. I usually walk to work. Today I _____ the bus.
12. The Smiths are home from vacation. I _____ them yesterday.
13. We _____ an important meeting yesterday. We elected a new company president.

B. Answer the questions about each picture. Use the past tense.

1. Did these people drive their cars to work? (take)
   No, they took the bus.
   Did Mrs. Smith stand on her way to work? (sit)
   Did Mr. King sit down? (stand)
2. How did Ms. Light get to Chicago? (fly)
   How did she get to the airport? (drive)
3. What happened to John? (break)
   How did he do this? (fall)
4. Did the children walk home from school? (run)

C. Read each sentence. Then form another sentence. Use the past tense and a time expression with **ago**.

Ex. This is my best drawing. (draw, several years)
I drew it several years ago.

1. "Starborn" is a good movie. (see, two nights)
2. My friend Charles is visiting me. (come, two days)
3. John has a broken arm. (fall, two weeks)
4. Jean is going to have a baby next June. (find out, two months)
5. Tom's mailing a letter. (write, two days)
6. I like that little car over there. (drive, a few days)
7. That was Mrs. Martin's favorite vase. (break, two days)
8. Captain Norris was a famous pilot. (fly, many years)

27 Past Tense: Summary of Regular and Irregular Verbs

cook	**cooked**	cut	**cut**
can	**canned**	come	**came**
copy	**copied**	catch	**caught**

A. Read each statement. Then answer the question. Use the past tense of the verb in the question. Also use one of the noun objects in parentheses.

Ex. Ned went to school. What did he ride? (a bicycle, a horse)
He rode a bicycle.

1. Jane was hungry. What did she think about? (food, home)
2. It was a cold night. What did Meredith want to protect? (the flowers, the ice)
3. She was away at college. Who did she miss? (her parents, her teacher)
4. He stepped on your foot. What did he say? (I'm sorry, thank you)
5. She was a language teacher. What did she teach? (Greek, history)
6. She was out of town. Where did she stay? (at home, in a hotel)
7. He's a good musician. What did he play? (cards, the piano)
8. His farm was in the north. What did he grow? (apples, oranges)
9. She worked on a farm. What did she drive? (a bus, a tractor)
10. He didn't know a word. What did he want? (a dictionary, a phone book)
11. The car had an accident. What did it hit? (a ball, a tree)
12. The bed was dirty. What did she change? (the rug, the sheets)
13. She needed a lot of money. What did she sell? (her pen, her watch)
14. He likes sports. What did he watch on TV? (a police story, a soccer game)
15. His pants are green. What did he sit on? (a rock, the grass)
16. Her friend was hungry. What did she give her? (her coat, her sandwich)
17. He made the dessert. What did he bring? (a cake, a salad)
18. He was shaving. What did he cut? (his face, his foot)
19. She changed her living room. What did she move? (the bed, the sofa)
20. It was almost noon and he was hungry. What did he eat? (lunch, tea)
21. A thief got in the jewelry store. What did he take? (some rings, some furs)

B. Study the calendar. Answer the questions with full sentences. Use the verb from the question.

Ex. On July 9 who did James Wilson meet at the airport?
He met Ted Long.

1. Did he meet him at National Airport?
2. When did Mr. Wilson have a luncheon appointment?
3. Who did he have lunch with?
4. Where did James go on Wednesday?
5. How did he get there?
6. When did he leave Chicago?
7. Who did he take to a movie?

JULY	JAMES WILSON—DAILY CALENDAR FENSTER ENGINEERING COMPANY • NEW YORK CITY			JULY
Monday	Tuesday	Wednesday	Thursday	Friday
9 9 a.m.: meet Ted Long Ames Airport	10 12:00 Lunch - Jim Weaver	11 7 a.m.: United Flight 401 - Chicago 10:00 Trade Building	12 1 p.m.: return on United #506	13 8 p.m.: pick up Jane - movie

28 Past Tense: Question Word Questions

Who } did Pat take?
What }

Where } did they go?
When }

A. Form a question about each sentence.

Ex. John taught at Harvard University. (What)
What did he teach?

1. I taught chemistry. (Where)
2. The ship returned safely. (When)
3. Pat did some work in the yard. (What)
4. The game ended early. (When)
5. Jerry lost his wallet. (Where)
6. Helen brought a friend to the party. (Who)
7. Mary heard a strange noise. (What)
8. My neighbor took a course at the college. (What)
9. Marie saw an old friend downtown. (Who)

B. Student 1: read the sentence. Student 2: ask a question about the underlined words. Student 1: then give a short answer.

Ex. The plane didn't arrive at <u>2:00</u>.
When did it arrive? At 3:00.

1. Dr. Forester didn't teach <u>at Washington University</u>.
2. We didn't eat <u>at Thompson's</u>.
3. I never drank <u>coffee</u> for breakfast in London.
4. Fred and Alice didn't meet <u>at school</u>.
5. I didn't study <u>math</u>.
6. The ship didn't sail from <u>Liverpool</u>.
7. Jane didn't wear <u>a dress</u> to the party.
8. Joan didn't tell <u>me</u> about it.
9. Classes didn't start <u>in September</u>.
10. Fred didn't take <u>Julia</u> to the dance.
11. I didn't say <u>"Help."</u>

C. Student 1: ask a question about each picture. Use **who, what, where,** or **when** and a verb on the list. Student 2: answer with a complete sentence.

| answer | do | land | ring |
| bring | eat | leave | take |

1. **When did the plane leave? It left at 2:00.**

29 Past Continuous: Affirmative and Negative

> She was/was not/wasn't working in the yard.
> We were/were not/weren't working downtown.

A. Form sentences like the model. Substitute the subject or the verb. Use **was** or **were**. Do 1-12 in order.

> He **was** learning English.

Ex. We
We were learning English.

1. Carlos
2. speak
3. The children
4. practice
5. I
6. use
7. They
8. read
9. write
10. You
11. Miss Osawa
12. teach

B. Form a negative sentence and an affirmative sentence like the example.

Ex. Randolph/earn $1200//earn $1400
Randolph wasn't earning $1200. He was earning $1400.

1. The tenants/waste gas//waste electricity
2. Julia/read a magazine//read a book
3. Mr. Harrison/sell washing machines//sell office machines
4. My father/look at the newspaper//take a nap
5. The Joneses/live in a house//live in an apartment
6. We/borrow money//lend it
7. Penny/write letters//make phone calls
8. You/manage the company//work for it
9. I/buy the house//rent it
10. Fred/pay cash//use a credit card
11. Mr. Michaels/save any money//spend it all

C. Study the pictures of members of the Foster family yesterday afternoon. Answer the questions with full sentences.

1. Was Billy sleeping at 3:30? **No, he wasn't sleeping. He was studying.**
   What was he doing at 5:30?
2. Was Mr. Foster leaving the office at 3:30?
   What was he doing at 5:30?
3. Was Anne studying at 3:30?
   What was she doing at 5:30?
4. What was Mrs. Foster doing at 3:30?
   Was she taking a nap at 5:30?
   What was she cooking for dinner?

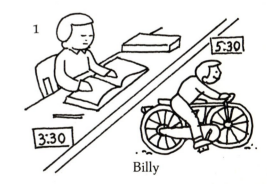
Billy

Mr. Foster

Anne

Mrs. Foster

30 Past Continuous: Questions and Short Answers

| Was | she | **playing?** | Yes, | she | **was.** |
| Were | you | **playing?** | No, | I | **wasn't.** |

A. Form sentences like the model. Substitute the subject or the verb. Use **was** or **were**. Do 1–12 in order.

<u>Was</u> <u>she</u> feeding the cat?

Ex. they
Were they feeding the cat?

1. follow
2. you
3. touch
4. he
5. hurt
6. I
7. both of you
8. the dogs
9. watch
10. your aunt
11. call
12. you and Helen

B. Student 1: ask a yes/no question. Student 2: give a short **yes** or **no** answer.

1. Mary/help the teacher//Yes
   Was Mary helping the teacher? Yes, she was.
2. He/sit on the ground//No
3. John/buy stamps//Yes
4. We/go to Chicago then//No
5. Mr. Florence/cash a check//Yes
6. You/deposit money//No
7. They/speak Italian//Yes
8. Your parents/work at the same company//No
9. The woman/lock the door//Yes
10. Harry/start a restaurant//No
11. The snow/cover the leaves in the road//Yes
12. The students/wait on the wrong corner//No

C. Student 1: ask yes/no questions about each picture. Use the past continuous verb form. Student 2: give a short **yes** or **no** answer. Then give a full sentence.

1. rain/yesterday afternoon
   Was it raining in St. Louis yesterday afternoon? Yes, it was. It was raining very hard.
2. work/last Tuesday afternoon
3. write/at 10:00 last night

31 Past Continuous Compared with Simple Past

I **saw** Mary downtown.
She **was shopping** for a coat.

A. Fill in the blanks with the verbs in the parentheses. Use the past continuous or simple past form.

1. I __saw__ a bear at the circus. It **was hugging** a clown. (hug, see)
2. I _____ a friend in the library. He _____ for a book about Greece. (look, meet)
3. I _____ Mother in the bedroom. She _____ a dress. (hear, sew)
4. Sue _____ into the kitchen. The potatoes _____. (burn, run)
5. She _____ a new coat. Her old one _____ out. (buy, wear)
6. She _____ an appointment at the doctor. Her leg _____. (hurt, make)
7. I _____ a noise downstairs. Jeanne _____ the piano. (hear, play)
8. He _____ out of the shower. The phone _____. (get, ring)
9. Jimmy _____ down the street. He _____ and _____ his arm. (fall, run, hurt)
10. My tooth _____. I _____ a piece of candy at the time. (break, chew)

B. Study the table. Form sentences about the train trip of the Ramelky family from Washington, D.C. to San Francisco, California. Use the time expressions and verbs like the example.

Ex. leave Washington/at 1:45 p.m.
They left Washington on the Broadway Limited at 1:45 p.m.

1. wait in Philadelphia/at 4:30 p.m.
2. sleep/at midnight
3. arrive in Chicago/on Thursday morning
4. spend Thursday/in Chicago
5. get on another train/at Chicago
6. cross the Mississippi River/at night
7. go across the plains/at ten o'clock Friday morning
8. be in Denver/at noon
9. cross the Rocky Mountains/between Cheyenne and Ogden
10. see the Sierra Nevadas/on Saturday
11. get to San Francisco/at 4:10 p.m. on Saturday

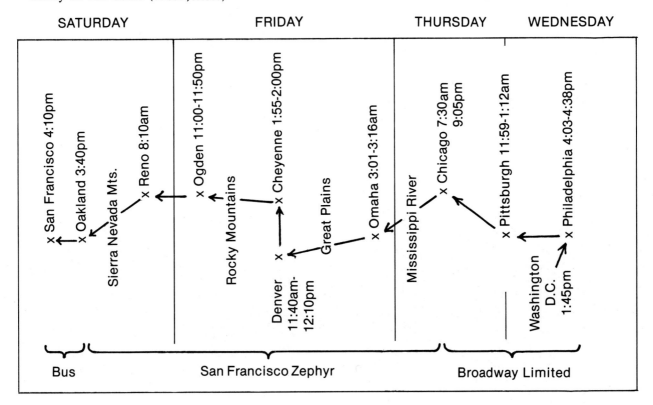

32 Future be going to: Affirmative and Negative

I **am/am not going** to ride today.
He **is/is not/isn't going** to ride today.
We **are/are not/aren't going** to ride today.

A. Form sentences like the model. Substitute the subject or the verb. Use the correct contracted form of **be**. Do 1–12 in order.

She's going to serve fish.

Ex. We
We're going to serve fish.

1. catch
2. He
3. eat
4. I
5. order
6. They
7. sell
8. The company
9. pack
10. You
11. cook
12. serve

B. Form a negative sentence and an affirmative sentence like the example.

Ex. Elena/play//work
Elena isn't going to play. She's going to work.

1. The children/ski//skate
2. We/eat potatoes//eat rice
3. Laura/write novels//write poems
4. Mrs. Wright/change the curtains//change the rug
5. Harry/pay the gas bill//pay the electric bill
6. Jenny/walk to work//take the bus
7. I/waste time//finish this work
8. The company/write them a letter//phone them
9. The bakers/use old eggs//get fresh ones
10. Dolly/sign her full name//use her initials
11. Lisa/leave the car on the street//park in the driveway

C. Form a negative sentence and an affirmative one about each picture.

1. Ted usually walks to work. John usually rides the bus.
   This morning Ted **isn't going to walk to work. He's going to take the bus.**
   John _____.

2. Mary usually plays cards in the afternoon. Alice usually swims.
   This afternoon, Mary _____.
   Alice _____.

3. The Martins usually go to Maine for their summer vacation. The Adamses usually go to the seashore for their vacation.
   This year the Martins _____.
   The Adamses _____.

33 Future be going to: Questions and Short Answers

Is he **going to** come?   Yes, he **is**.
Are they **going to** come?   No, they **aren't**.
Are you **going to** come?   No, I'm **not**.

A. Form sentences like the model. Substitute the subject, the verb, or the object. Use **are** or **is**. Do 1–12 in order.

    <u>Are</u> <u>you</u> going to <u>paint</u> <u>the garage</u>?

Ex. the house
    Are you going to paint the house?

1. she
2. they
3. fix up
4. the car
5. sell
6. Alice
7. Bill
8. return
9. the library books
10. they
11. the money
12. the insurance company

B. Student 1: ask a yes/no question. Student 2: give a short **yes** or **no** answer.

Ex. those birds//go south//Yes
    Are those birds going to go south?
    Yes, they are.

1. he/get well//No
2. the tea/cool off//Yes
3. water/get in the basement//No
4. Judith/get married soon//Yes
5. it/rain this afternoon//No
6. coal/go up in price//Yes
7. you/use your best dishes//Yes
8. the children/read comic books//No
9. you/wear a sweater//Yes
10. Mr. Longworth/buy that company//No
11. We/stop for lunch soon//Yes

C. Student 1: ask a yes/no question about events on the sports schedule. Student 2: give a short answer. Then give a full sentence.

Ex. A. Are the Titans going to play basketball on Wednesday? Yes, they are. They're going to play the Rockets.

Ex. B. Are they going to play volleyball on the eighth? No, they aren't. They're not going to play that day.

MARCH SPORTS SCHEDULE

Wednesday	Thursday	Friday	Saturday
1/ Basketball Titans vs. Rockets 7 p.m.	2/ Tennis 1st Round 2 p.m. CANCELLED	3/ Basketball Eagles vs. Jays 7 p.m.	4/ Swimming Meet 2:30 p.m.
8/ Volleyball Blues vs. Reds 7 p.m. CANCELLED	9/ Tennis Finals 2 p.m. CANCELLED	10/ Bicycle Racing 2 p.m.	11/ Boxing Jones vs. Herrera 9 p.m.

34 Future will: Affirmative and Negative

We **will** begin.	We **will not** begin.
He**'ll** go back.	He **won't** go back.

A. Form sentences like the model. Substitute the subject or the verb. Do 1–12 in order.

That will be good.

Ex. I
I will be good.

1. She
2. look
3. You
4. Stan and he
5. feel
6. I
7. It
8. smell
9. sound
10. The car
11. Her English
12. Your voice

B. Form a negative sentence and an affirmative sentence. Use **will** (or **'ll**) and **won't**.

Ex. I/take Route 66//take Route 80
I won't take Route 66. I'll take Route 80.

1. I/take Spanish//take German
2. She/wear a skirt//wear jeans
3. She/talk to her mother//talk to her aunt
4. The company/raise the price//make a small package
5. They/mail the package//deliver it by truck
6. Mr. Steger/forget you//call you tomorrow morning
7. The wedding/be cheap//cost $2,000
8. Mrs. Gordon/call her daughter tonight//call her first thing in the morning
9. These watches/break down easily//give years of service
10. The weather/improve//be this way all week
11. Miss Baker/buy a new car this year//drive the old one

C. Form a negative and an affirmative sentence about each picture.

1. (at eight//at nine)
 **The bank won't open at eight.
 It'll open at nine.**
2. (to Paris//to Madrid)
3. (the car//the motorcycle)
4. ($250//$300)

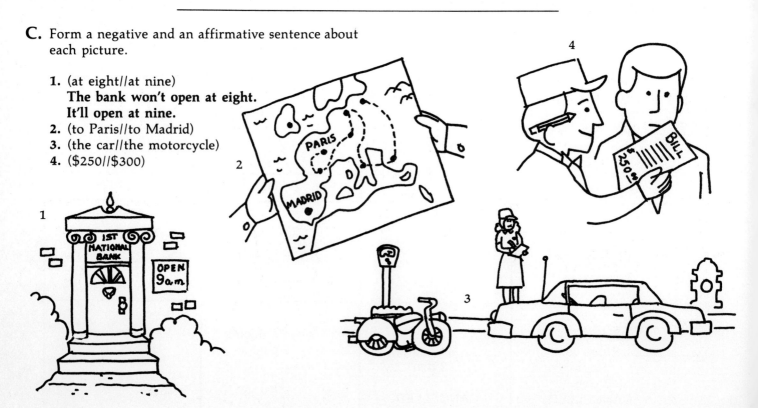

35 Future will: Questions and Short Answers

Will she **be** there? Yes, she **will**.
Will you **be** glad? No, I **won't**.

A. Form sentences like the model. Substitute the subject and the verb. Do 1–12 in order.

Will <u>she</u> <u>eat</u> lunch?

Ex. they
Will they eat lunch?

1. pack
2. he
3. you
4. carry
5. Mr. Williams
6. the children
7. buy
8. your boss
9. make
10. we
11. need
12. I

B. Student 1: ask a yes/no question. Student 2: give a short **yes** or **no** answer.

Ex. this rain/stop soon//Yes
Will this rain stop soon? Yes, it will.

1. she/eat the peaches//Yes
2. the scissors/cut this box//No
3. Donald/sit in that seat//Yes
4. your uncle/bring his guitar//No
5. the eggs/be safe//Yes
6. the flag/stay up all night//No
7. Patty/answer the phone//Yes
8. her cousin/be out of town//No
9. those books/cost fifteen dollars//Yes
10. these tires/go 30,000 miles//No

C. Student 1: ask yes/no questions about each picture. Use the verbs in each list. Student 2: give a short **yes** or **no** answer.

1. Will Flight 606 from Boston be on time?
   No, it won't.
2. Will the fireman climb the ladder?
   Yes, he will.

1

2

climb/jump/put/put out/save

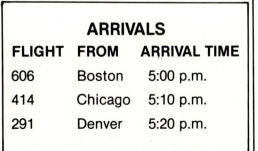

ARRIVALS		
FLIGHT	FROM	ARRIVAL TIME
606	Boston	5:00 p.m.
414	Chicago	5:10 p.m.
291	Denver	5:20 p.m.

arrive/be/come in/land

36 Future: Question Word Questions

Who } is Pat going to take?
What }

Where } will they go?
When }

A. Student 1: ask a question word question. Use **will**.
Student 2: give a short answer. Use the words.

Ex. When/I/see/you/again?//1:00 Tuesday
When will I see you again? At 1:00 Tuesday.

1. Where/we/meet?//restaurant/16th Street
2. Who/we/invite/party?//Jim,Bill,Ted,Alice
3. What/she/tell/Jim?//truth
4. When/wedding/take place?//June 6
5. Where/wedding/be?//St. Michael's Church
6. When/they/pay bill?//first/next month
7. Where/meeting/be held?//Room 607
8. Who/meet/us/airport?//tour director
9. What/I give/Mary/birthday?//watch

B. Student 1: ask question word questions about Mrs. Jones's schedule. Use **be going to**. Student 2: answer with a full sentence.

Ex. A. When is Mrs. Jones going to do her wash?
She's going to do it at 9:00 on Monday morning.
Ex. B. What is she going to buy at the hardware store?
She's going to buy some grass seed and two batteries.

HELEN A. JONES

APPOINTMENTS		SHOPPING LIST	

Monday, May 6	9:00 wash
	10:30 call June
	12:30 lunch with Florence – El Patio Restaurant
	5:00 pick up Ted at bus station
		Groceries
		  milk
		  hamburger
		  onions
		Drug store
		  toothpaste
		Hardware
		  grass seed
			lettuce
			ice cream
			
			aspirin
			
			2 batteries

Tuesday, May 7	9-12 housework - beds - clean - dishes
	2:00 tennis with Joyce
	5:30 pick up Ted at office
		Bakery
		  bread
		Bank
		  deposit check
			doz. hamburger buns
			
			pay electric bill

Wednesday, May 8	10-12 shopping with Edith	Cleaners
		  take Ted's jacket
		  pick up cleaning	

37 Future: Summary

The Eagles	**are going to play**	tomorrow.
The Giants	**will play**	tomorrow.
The Tigers	**are playing**	tomorrow.
The Yankees	**play**	tomorrow.

A. Study the schedule. Student 1: ask **when** questions like the examples. Use the present verb tense form. Student 2: answer with a full sentence.

Ex. A. When do the Eagles play the Giants? They play them on Sunday, June 1.
Ex. B. When do the Tigers and the Cardinals play? They play on June 5.

Do the drill again, but use the present continuous tense.

Ex. When are the Lions playing the Tigers? They're playing them on the ninth.

LOCAL BASEBALL SCHEDULE

MONDAY	TUESDAY	WEDNESDAY	THURSDAY	FRIDAY	SATURDAY	SUNDAY
-1-	-2-	-3-	-4-	-5-	-6-	-7-
Eagles vs. Giants	Tigers vs. Yankees	Lions vs. Bears	White Sox vs. Penguins	Tigers vs. Cardinals	Eagles vs. Tigers	Yankees vs. Giants
-8-	-9-	-10-	-11-	-12-	-13-	-14-
Penguins vs. Cardinals	Lions vs. Tigers	Bears vs. Giants	Eagles vs. Yankees	Tigers vs. White Sox	Cardinals vs. Giants	Yankees vs. Bears

B. Student 1: ask a yes/no question. Put the sentence parts in the correct order. Student 2: answer with **no** and a full sentence. Use information in a–j.

1. take French/you/will/next year?
2. is/going to/Georgie/be/an engineer?
3. will/in the fall/your daughter/get a job?
4. are/taking/the 9:00 flight/you/tomorrow?
5. you/are going to/this year/buy a house?
6. be/the wedding/cheap/will?
7. be/next year at this time/will/in Europe/you?
8. are going to/you/stay home/tonight?
9. save her allowance/Annie/is going to?
10. be/will/interesting/the meeting?

a. stay in our apartment
b. very expensive
c. take German
d. go to the library and study
e. spend it
f. go to college
g. be right here
h. writer
i. the 8:00 flight
j. boring as usual

Will you take French next year?
No, I'll take German.

38 Auxiliary can

| She **can** drive.
He **can't** drive. | **Can** you drive? | Yes, I **can**.
No, I **can't**. |

A. Form an affirmative and a negative sentence like the example. Use **can** and **can't**.

Ex. She/swim//dive
She can swim. She can't dive.

1. He/skate//ski
2. She/play cards//play chess
3. He/play the piano//play the guitar
4. I/fix radios//fix TVs
5. you/see the moon//see any stars
6. We/go to the zoo//go to the museum
7. They/change the oil//change the tires
8. Paul/speak English//speak Arabic
9. Maria/shut the window//lock it
10. Tom/spend money//save it
11. Miss Neuman/type well//take dictation

B. Student 1: ask a yes/no question. Use **can**. Student 2: give a short answer.

Ex. you/see the airplane//No
Can you see the airplane? No, I can't.

1. you/hear the phone//Yes
2. he/lift that chair//No
3. she/run up the stairs//Yes
4. they/come tomorrow//No
5. they/sell those bicycles//Yes
6. you/read/with your glasses off//No
7. she/make her own dresses//No
8. Mr. Schlieper/afford new clothes//No
9. you/buy a hot dog//Yes
10. you/understand her lecture//No
11. horses/swim//Yes

C. Student 1: ask a yes/no question about each picture. Use **can**. Student 2: give a short **yes** or **no** answer.

1. **Can that man hear the phone?**
   No, he can't. He's deaf. (or) **He can't hear well.**

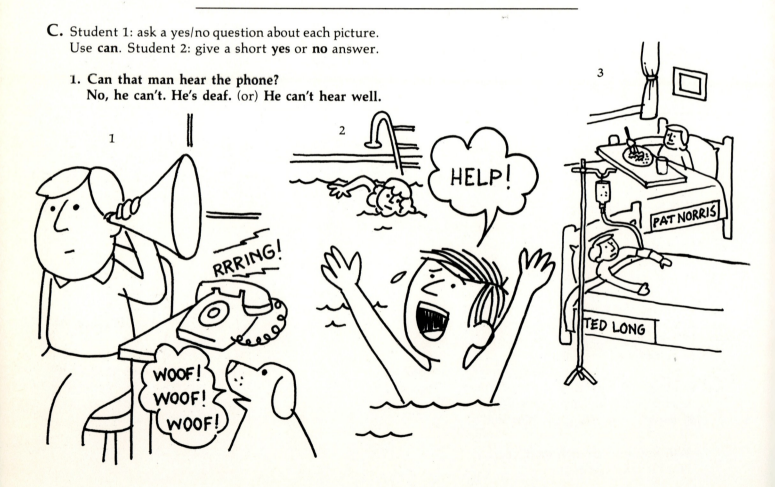

39 Verbs have and want + Infinitive

> She **has to work.**   Does she **have to work?**   Yes, she does.
> I **don't want to go.**   Do you **want to go?**   No, I don't.

A. Form sentences like the model. Substitute the subject, the verb, or the infinitive. Do 1–12 in order.

<u>He</u> <u>has</u> to <u>walk</u> home.

Ex. I
I have to walk home.

1. be
2. You
3. want
4. stay
5. We
6. don't want
7. She
8. They
9. I
10. don't have
11. John
12. leave

B. Student 1: ask a yes/no question. Use **you** as the subject. Student 2: give a short **yes** or **no** answer.

Ex. want/take a bath//Yes
Do you want to take a bath? Yes, I do.

1. have/stay in bed//Yes
2. want/play basketball//No
3. have/pay now//No
4. want/take off your sweater//Yes
5. have/paint the house today//Yes
6. want/see my stamp collection//No
7. have/make an appointment//Yes
8. want/sell some jewelry//Yes
9. have/get a new winter coat//Yes
10. want/march in the parade//No
11. have/go to the dentist again//No

C. Student 1: ask a yes/no question. Use the verb **want to**. Student 2: answer with **Yes, but** and a full sentence. Use the verb **have to**.

1. **Do they want to turn left?**
   Yes, but they have to go straight ahead.

40 Summary of Verb Forms

> hold holds holding held
> look looks looking looked

A. Complete the table. Fill in the missing plain, present -s, continuous -ing, and past tense forms.

#	plain	-s	-ing	past
1.	work	works	working	worked
2.	stop			
3.		reads		
4.			buying	
5.				began
6.	send			
7.		wins		
8.			having	
9.				drove

B. Fill in the blanks with a verb form from the parentheses.

1. What does Mr. Johnson do?
   He **teaches** English. (teach, teaches)
2. What did Miss Marston do?
   She _____ the class schedules. (make, made)
3. What are those dogs doing?
   They're _____ at that cat. (bark, barking)
4. What will you do tomorrow?
   I'll _____ my friends in Chicago. (visit, visiting)
5. What was Mildred doing at the store?
   She was _____ on the new dresses. (tried, trying)
6. When will he take care of this bill?
   He'll have to _____ it next week. (pay, pays)

C. Fill in the blanks with another form of the underlined verb.

1. We <u>ran</u> into the house. A dog was **running** after us.
2. Many children <u>eat</u> at noon. They're _____ lunch in the cafeteria now.
3. I <u>own</u> a Japanese car, and Miss Sudoh _____ an American one.
4. I usually <u>watch</u> the news on TV at 11:00, but I _____ a movie last night.
5. I <u>saw</u> the play last night. When will you _____ it?
6. Betty doesn't <u>walk</u> often, but she _____ to school yesterday.
7. The skis <u>cost</u> $65 and the jacket _____ $35.
8. Flight 507 usually <u>arrives</u> at 5:05, but it's _____ early today.

41 Summary of Negative Sentences

They	**aren't**	swimming.
She	**didn't**	like the roses.
I	**can't**	come today.

A. Respond to the statements like the examples. Use a short negative sentence and a full negative sentence with **either**.

Ex. A. Al drives a truck. (Art//a car)
Art doesn't. He doesn't drive a car either.
Ex. B. Barbara swam in the first race. (Betty//in the second race)
Betty didn't. She didn't swim in the second race either.

1. Dolly was in the garden. (Debbie//in the garage)
2. Ed can play the guitar. (Eric//the piano)
3. Fran will graduate in June. (Flo//in January)
4. Gil is taking Russian. (Gary//German)
5. Joan writes a lot of letters. (Her husband//postcards)
6. I saw the accident. (The policeman//the fight)
7. He's a good musician. (His friend//a good writer)
8. We were on time for Paul's speech. (Mr. Gale//Ted's speech)
9. Helen's going to be there. (Heather//here)
10. Jack was studying upstairs. (Jim//at the library)
11. Al and Art drive motorcycles. (Ann and Alice//trucks)
12. Barbara and Betty swam on Saturday. (Bob and Bill//on Sunday)
13. Dolly and Debbie were in that class. (Don and Dave//my math class)
14. Mark and Mel are studying foreign languages. (Mary and Monica//math)
15. The Tigers have a good goalie. (The Eagles//a good coach)

B. Study the picture. Form negative sentences about subjects 1-6. Use the contractions **isn't, aren't, doesn't, don't, can't,** and **won't**.

1. The traffic lights
2. The traffic
3. The policeman
4. That businessman
5. Burgerworld
6. The window washer

1. **The traffic lights aren't working.** (or) **The traffic lights don't work.**

42 Summary of Yes/No Questions and Short Answers

Is	he	**running**?	Yes,	he	**is.**
Did	she	**like** roses?	No,	she	**didn't.**
Will	you	**come** today?	No,	I	**won't.**

A. Student 1: ask two yes/no questions about each picture. Student 2: give short **yes** or **no** answers.

1. Are _____? (ski//bobsled)
   Are they skiing? No, they aren't.
   Are they bobsledding? Yes, they are.
2. Did _____? (play hockey//slalom)
3. Does _____? (slalom//ski jump)
4. Is _____? (ski//speed skate)
5. Were _____? (speed skate//figure skate)
6. Will _____? (bobsled//play hockey)

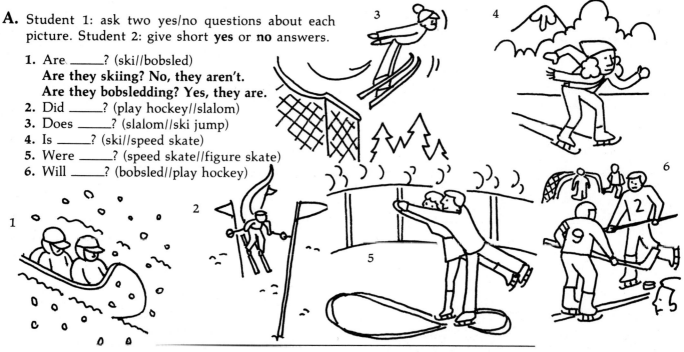

B. It's February 9th. Laura and Nick marked their favorite events on the program. Student 1: form yes/no questions like the examples. Student 2: give short answers according to the program.

Ex. A. Is Nick watching a hockey game now? No, he isn't.
Ex. B. Did Laura and Nick go to the opening ceremony? Yes, they did.
Ex. C. Will women's figure skating begin on Wednesday? No, it won't.

	NORTH COUNTRY WINTER GAMES February 7-10							
SUNDAY-7	MONDAY-8		TUESDAY-9		WEDNESDAY-10	
Opening Ceremony (a) (L,N)	Bobsled (e)	(N)	Slalom (d)	(L,N)	Ski Jumping (d)	(N,L)
	Figure Skating — Men (c)	( )	Figure Skating — Women (c)	(L)	Figure Skating — Pairs (c)	(L)
	Speed Skating — Women (b)	(L)	Speed Skating — Men (b)	(N)	Cross Country Skiing (e)	( )
	Ice Hockey (a)	(N,L)	Ice Hockey (a)	( )	Ice Hockey (a)	(N)
LOCATIONS:	(a) Knudsen Arena (b) Lake Heiden		(c) Sonja Rink (d) Mt. Killy		(e) Mt. Oleg	

SECTION TWO

43 Nouns: Uses of Nouns

This **room** is the **bedroom**.
A **child** is eating **candy** in the **bedroom**.

A. Fill in the blanks with the nouns in parentheses.

1. A __rose__ is a __flower__. (flower, rose)
2. A _____ is a _____. (bird, chicken)
3. _____ is _____. (bread, food)
4. _____ is a _____. (liquid, water)
5. This _____ is a _____. (building, school)
6. That _____ is a _____. (coin, quarter)
7. This _____ is a _____. (book, dictionary)
8. That _____ is _____. (Main Street, street)
9. _____ is my _____. (Mary, sister)
10. This _____ will be my _____. (birthday, Friday)
11. Our _____ is a _____. (teacher, neighbor)
12. His _____ was _____. (cotton, shirt)

B. Study the picture. Fill in the blanks with nouns from the list.

bear   car   ground   man   table   tent
cap   child hand   stick   tea   tree

1. A __bear__ is in the __tent__.
2. A _____ is lying by the _____.
3. The _____ spilled on the _____.
4. The _____ is up in the _____.
5. A _____ is in his _____.
6. The _____ is in the _____.

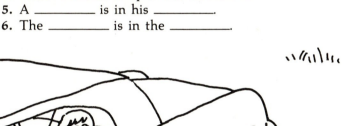

C. Form sentences like the model. Substitute the nouns in the correct order.

The <u>clerk</u> put the <u>package</u> on the <u>shelf</u>.

Ex. counter/customer/hat
    The customer put the hat on the counter.

1. letter/mailman/table
2. counter/lady/money
3. cashier/change/counter
4. picture/student/wall
5. man/toothbrush/toothpaste
6. boy/kite/tail
7. doll/dress/girl
8. waiter/fish/lemon
9. bread/child/jelly
10. food/table/waiter

44 Nouns: Regular Plural Forms

pen	**pens**	/z/*
pipe	**pipes**	/s/
peach	**peaches**	/ɪz/

A. Form the plural of these nouns. Give the correct sound of the ending: /z/, /s/, or /ɪz/.

Ex. bag
    bags /z/

1. book	6. ear	11. page	16. tape
2. bowl	7. gun	12. piece	17. thing
3. moth	8. hat	13. road	18. tub
4. day	9. name	14. safe	19. watch
5. dish	10. nose	15. stove	

B. Fill in the blanks with the plural forms of the nouns. State which plural form you used: /z/, /s/, or /ɪz/.

1. We learned long <u>lists</u>/s/ of <u>verbs</u>/z/ . (list, verb)
2. The _____ watched two _____. (film, girl)
3. The _____ have clean _____. (hand, nurse)
4. The _____ will grow in two _____. (month, plant)
5. The _____ had several _____. (part, test)
6. Those _____ need new _____. (bulb, lamp)
7. These _____ have more than 300 _____. (book, page)
8. Those _____ have white _____. (barn, farm)
9. These _____ have strong _____. (fence, field)
10. They made some _____ in the _____. (change, word)
11. The city has green _____ and old _____. (church, park)
12. The _____ are giving away _____. (bank, gift)

C. Make sentences about the pictures. Use the plural form of nouns from the list.

collar	garage	pencil	ticket
eraser	movie	puppy	window

1. He has tickets for two movies.

*The symbols within / / represent **sounds**, not spelling.

45 Nouns: Irregular Plural Forms

child	**children**	wife	**wives**
foot	**feet**	path/θ/*	**paths**/ðz/

A. Label the pictures. Use the number and the plural form of a noun from the list.

fish   half   loaf   mouse
foot   knife   man   wolf

1. two feet

B. Fill in the blanks with the plural form of the nouns from the list.

child   goose   life   sheep   thief   wife
deer   leaf   mouth   shelf   tooth   woman

1. The baby's getting several new ___teeth___.
2. I need more _____ for my books.
3. Two _____ left their handbags on the bus.
4. The Burtons have two _____—a boy and a girl.
5. The police are looking for three _____.
6. Some people say that cats have nine _____.
7. The Burtons have 50 _____ and 200 _____ on their farm.
8. _____ are eating _____ off those trees.
9. Tom and Bob gave their _____ new coats.
10. The boys put candy in their _____.

C. Student 1: ask a question like the model. Substitute a noun in the question. Student 2: answer the question. Use the plural form of the noun.

Do you see a <u>thief</u>? No, I see two <u>thieves</u>.

Ex. man
Do you see a man? No, I see two men.

1. mouse   4. child   7. wolf
2. fish   5. woman   8. foot
3. tooth   6. calf   9. path

*The symbols within // represent **sounds**, not spelling.

46 Nouns: Singular vs. Plural Nouns

one **hand**
two **hands**

A. Substitute the word before **egg**. Use the singular (**egg**) or plural (**eggs**) form. Sometimes you can use **egg** or **eggs**.

He ate an egg.

Ex. a few
He ate a few eggs.

1. a lot of
2. another
3. each
4. eight
5. every
6. her
7. his
8. many
9. my
10. no
11. one
12. our
13. some
14. that
15. the
16. their
17. the other
18. these
19. this
20. those
21. your

B. Fill in the blanks with the nouns in parentheses. Use the singular or plural form.

1. We didn't wash the __dishes__ after **breakfast**. (breakfast, dish)
2. We gave our _____ to the _____. (teacher, test)
3. She counted six _____ in the _____ "yellow." (letter, word)
4. She sewed the _____ on her new _____ last. (dress, sleeve)
5. He ate a _____ of _____. (box, nut)
6. He washed the _____ and _____ of the car. (roof, window)
7. They put their _____ in that _____. (closet, coat)
8. They left the _____ in the _____. (hotel, key)
9. The program lasted an _____ and thirty _____. (hour, minute)
10. Mary cooked the _____ and _____. (chicken, vegetable)
11. Gary drew _____ on the front _____. (door, picture)
12. This _____ sells _____. (cigarette, machine)

C. Study the pictures. Student 1: ask a question like the model. Use the singular or plural form of the noun. Student 2: answer the question.

What has fifty-two weeks? A year.

Ex. 1/eye
What has one eye? A needle.

1. 7/day
2. 3/side
3. 2/wing
4. 2/wheel
5. 4/leg
6. 6/pocket

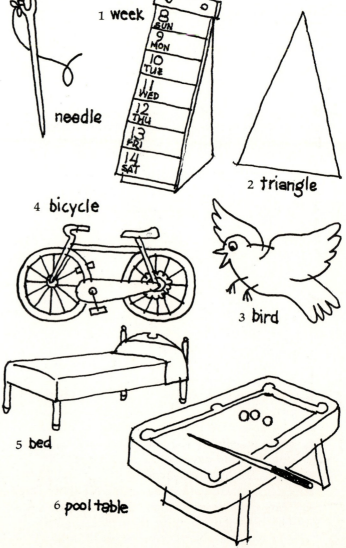

1 week
needle
2 triangle
3 bird
4 bicycle
5 bed
6 pool table

47 Nouns: Countable vs. Noncountable Nouns

cows	beef
some cows	some beef
a cow	a piece of beef

A. Match each noun with an adjective. Then form a sentence like the example. (Use the plural form of all the countable nouns.)

1. balloon
2. cigarette
3. clothing
4. milk
5. party
6. snow
7. candy
8. big word

a. cold
b. delicious
c. difficult
d. expensive now
e. fun
f. harmful
g. round
h. sweet

1. **Balloons are round.**

B. Student 1: ask a question like the model. Substitute one of the nouns. Student 2: answer the question. Use a different noun.

Did Mike want some <u>beans</u>?
No, he wanted some <u>bread</u>.

Ex. meat//vegetable
Did Mike want some meat?
No, he wanted some vegetables.

1. match//wood
2. bag//string
3. paper//pencil
4. gas//tire
5. comb//toothpaste
6. information//money
7. book//music
8. film//stamp
9. water//water glass
10. corn//tomato
11. rock//sand

C. Study the pictures. Complete the sentences. Use **a/an** with countable nouns. Use **a bag of, a drop of, a box of, a piece of** with uncountable nouns.

1. She bought <u>a bag of flour</u>.
2. MacPherson picked _____.
3. He didn't drink _____.
4. She left _____.
5. I found _____.
6. The boy wants _____.

48 Nouns: Possessive Forms

son's	/z/*	sons'	/z/
aunt's	/s/	aunts'	/s/
niece's	/ɪz/	nieces'	/ɪz/

A. Form the possessive of these nouns. Give the sound of the possessive ending: /z/, /s/, or /ɪz/.

1. a bear's ears /z/
2. a duck__ feathers / /
3. a fish__ eyes / /
4. a mouse__ fur / /
5. a pig__ skin / /
6. a whale__ tail / /
7. a wolf__ teeth / /
8. Butch__ lunch / /
9. Debbie__ baby / /
10. Jake__ bike / /
11. Pam__ room / /
12. Robert__ hat / /
13. Miss Long__ tongue / /
14. Mr. Page__ age / /

B. Form noun phrases like the example. Use the possessive form of one of the plural nouns.

Ex. birds/wings
    birds' wings

1. money/people
2. buses/wheels
3. sheep/wool
4. countries/flags
5. uniforms/waitresses
6. pay/workers
7. beds/children
8. parks/trees
9. bank account/Chatmans
10. teeth/whales
11. microphones/speakers

C. Study the pictures. Fill in the blanks with nouns from the list. Use the singular or plural possessive form.

car   cat   nurse   player   student   uncle

1. The **student's** hands were covered with chalk.
2. The _____ uniforms were all dirty.
3. The _____ tires are new.
4. The baby likes to touch the _____ fur.
5. The _____ feet need a rest.
6. Seymour was my _____ only lawyer.

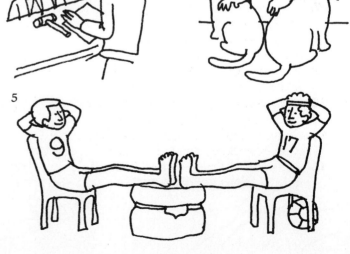

*The symbols within // represent **sounds**, not spelling.

49 Nouns: Summary of Forms

| parent | parent's | parents | parents' |
| child | child's | children | children's |

A. Complete the table. Fill in the missing singular, singular possessive, plural, and plural possessive forms.

1. hand	hand's	hands	hands'
2.	pilot's		
3.		wives	
4. mouse			
5.	boss's		
6.		babies	

B. Fill in the blanks with a noun form from the parentheses.

1. Whose book is this? It's the **teacher's**. (teacher's, teachers)
2. Whose toothbrush is that? It's my _____. (sister's, sisters')
3. Whose lunch boxes are those? They're the _____. (worker's, workers')
4. What do they sell there? They sell _____. (flower, flowers)
5. What did the children laugh at? The funny _____. (clowns, clowns')
6. What did you buy? A pair of _____. (shoe, shoes)
7. Who owns this tent? It's the _____. (circus's, circuses)
8. Who uses this book? The _____. (teacher, teacher's)
9. Who left these shoes here? The _____. (children, children's)
10. Whose children are those? They're that _____. (woman's, women's)
11. Did you call your sister? No, the _____ wasn't working. (phone, phones)
12. Did she want to be a nurse? No, a _____ life is hard. (nurse, nurse's)

C. Fill in the blanks with another form of the underlined noun.

1. Mr. Kidd has a <u>son</u> in the army and two __sons__ in the navy.
2. Our <u>family</u> ate lunch in the park. Many _____ were there.
3. A <u>woman</u> asked the clerk, "Where do you have _____ hats?"
4. <u>Herb</u> and Oliver have new bikes. _____ bike is green.
5. Your <u>teacher</u> is not in school. She's at a _____ meeting today.
6. My <u>wife</u> wants to go to the party. Many _____ don't want to go.
7. I called a <u>taxi</u> for 4:00. At 4:05, three _____ came.
8. The <u>boss</u> will be here soon. Don't sit there; that's the _____ chair.
9. Today is <u>Sunday</u>. This month has five _____.
10. A ball hit him in the <u>teeth</u>. One _____ was broken.
11. One <u>farmer's</u> house was on fire. All the other _____ helped him.
12. He has fourteen <u>cows</u>. One _____ leg is broken.

50 Article a vs. an

a lemon
an orange

A. Form sentences like the model. Use a noun and **a** or **an**.

That looks like **a** lake.

Ex. ant
That looks like an ant.

1. bottle
2. car
3. door
4. egg
5. farm
6. gate
7. horse
8. island
9. jar
10. kite
11. lion
12. match
13. nut
14. onion
15. penny
16. quarter
17. river
18. sandwich
19. ship
20. tape
21. umbrella
22. uniform
23. vase
24. wagon
25. yard
26. zoo

B. Form new sentences like the example. Use the adjective in parentheses and **a** or **an**.

Ex. We had a lesson today. (easy)
We had an easy lesson today.

1. We had a test today. (hard)
2. Javier is a child. (active)
3. Javier is an artist. (young)
4. Sandy is a student. (honest)
5. It was a message. (unhappy)
6. I saw an accident. (strange)
7. She's wearing a hat. (old)
8. We're having a meeting. (quick)
9. Sandy took a train. (early)
10. I heard a speech. (interesting)
11. It was a trip. (useful)
12. That's an oven. (hot)

C. Study the pictures. Fill in the blanks with **a** or **an** and a noun.

1. He hurt **an arm** and **a leg**.
2. She's _____ and _____.
3. This story's about _____ and _____.
4. I need _____ and _____.
5. She offered me _____ and _____.
6. He took _____ in _____.

2 painter/teacher
6 ride/airplane

51 Article *the*: Uses of *the*

The moon is behind clouds.
She's a good player, but she's not **the only good player**.
I bought a radio. **The radio** doesn't work.

A. Fill in the blanks with **the** and a noun from the list.

| driver | left | living room | receptionist |
| guitar | library | radio | sun |

1. He plays **the guitar** very well.
2. I heard about it on _____.
3. Miss Corda borrowed five books from _____.
4. Our house is on this road on _____.
5. I need dark glasses. _____ is very bright.
6. Kay got in the taxi. She gave directions to _____.
7. Kay's home. She's in _____.
8. I got to the office at 9:00. I gave my name to _____.

B. Fill in the blanks with **a/an** or **the** and one of the adjectives in parentheses.

1. Jackie is **the youngest** member. (young, youngest)
2. Jay and Kay were born on _____ day. (new, same)
3. Some flowers bloom in April, _____ month. (fourth, warm)
4. Miss Murphy is _____ American in the class. (cold, only)
5. _____ storm was in January. (bad, worst)
6. A good map is on _____ page. (different, next)
7. She took _____ road and got lost. (fast, wrong)
8. _____ plane left at 11:45 p.m. (long, last)

C. Study the pictures and answer the questions. Use **the** instead of **a** in the answers.

1. Did a page come out of the book?
   Yes, the page with Washington on it.
2. Did we get a bill today?
3. Is there a call for Bill?
4. Are they going to have a meeting?
5. "Is there a telephone here?"

52 Article a/an vs. the

I found **a** coin.
The coin was old.

A. Form two sentences like the example. Use **a/an** in the first and **the** in the second.

  Ex. buy/lamp//switch/broken
  I bought a lamp. The switch was broken.

  1. borrow/book//cover/dirty
  2. visit/farm//animals/healthy
  3. look at/house//kitchen/too small
  4. use/pen//ink/too light
  5. carry/handbag//strap/very long
  6. take/exam//room/very quiet
  7. buy/clock//alarm/very loud
  8. have/bicycle//seat/too high
  9. read/article//subject/interesting

B. Fill in the blanks with **a/an** or **the**.

  1. This paper cost only ___**a**___ dollar.
  2. Did you throw _____ garbage in _____ waste basket?
  3. [wife to husband] How much was _____ hotel bill?
  4. I need _____ application form.
  5. [passenger to airline clerk] When will we get on _____ plane?
  6. [caller to phone operator] I'm making _____ long distance call.
  7. He lived in Spain for five years, but he never learned _____ language.
  8. [father to daughter] What was _____ score of _____ game today?
  9. I'm going to _____ library for _____ book about taxes.
  10. That man plays _____ violin in _____ famous orchestra.
  11. We just saw _____ fire across _____ street. We called _____ fire department.
  12. _____ president is giving _____ speech about _____ war.

C. Study the pictures. Then answer the questions. Use **a/an** in one sentence and **the** in the other.

  1. Do you want an umbrella or a raincoat?
  I'll take an umbrella. I don't want the raincoat.
  2. Do you want any fruit?
  3. Would you like a cup or a glass?
  4. Which seat would you like?

53 Modifiers and Substitutes: Possessive Nouns

Is this **John's** tape? No, it's **Mary's**.
I hear a **boy's** voice and a **girl's**.

A. Form sentences like the model. Use the possessive form of the nouns.

I'll write the <u>boy's</u> name and the <u>girl's</u>.

Ex. nurse/doctor
I'll write the nurse's name and the doctor's.

1. parent/child
2. boss/secretary
3. teacher/student
4. lawyer/judge
5. police officer/thief
6. company/president
7. hunter/dog
8. town/street
9. waiter/cashier

B. Study the table. Student 1: ask questions like the example. Use a possessive modifier. Student 2: answer the question. Use a possessive substitute.

Ex. Rose/Dick/sister
Is Rose Dick's sister?
No, she's Ray's and Ruth's.

1. Dawn/Max and Eve/daughter
2. Eve/Bob/wife
3. Doug/Hope/husband
4. Dick/Ruth/brother
5. Ray/Bob and Hope/son
6. Max/Dick/father
7. Eve/Dawn/mother

C. Answer the questions like the examples. Use the information in parentheses and a possessive modifier or substitute.

Ex. A. Is this your dictionary? (my roommate)
No, it's my roommate's.

Ex. B. Were they your parents? (cousins/my roommate)
No, they were my roommate's cousins.

1. Is this your address? (Mike)
2. Are these your glasses? (Mary)
3. Are these your shoes? (slippers/my son)
4. Was that your fault? (the typist)
5. Are those your shirts? (dresses/my wife)
6. Is he the owner? (brother/the manager)

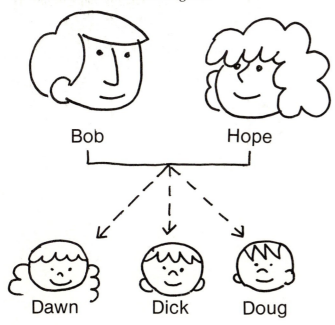
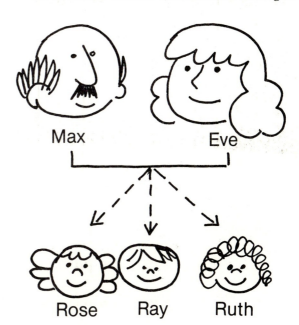

54 Modifiers and Substitutes: Adjectives and Adjective + one

This is a **good** egg. That isn't a **good one**.
These are **good** eggs. Those aren't **good ones**.

A. Answer the question like the example. Use the noun in parentheses.

Ex. Does Art have a new car? (motorcycle)
No, he has a new motorcycle.

1. Does Art have a big house? (bank account)
2. Does Art have a good calculator? (typewriter)
3. Do they make good shirts? (jeans)
4. Did they serve hot chocolate? (coffee)
5. Did she use sharp knives? (scissors)
6. Did she pick the ripe tomatoes? (cucumbers)
7. Is he wearing a blue suit? (sweater)
8. Is she eating a sour grape? (peach)
9. Was it a windy day? (night)
10. Are they washing the dirty bus? (truck)
11. Did they sell the old boat? (plane)

B. Answer the question like the example. Use the adjective in parentheses and **one** or **ones**.

Ex. Do you have a new car? (old)
No, I have an old one.

1. Do you have a large garden? (small)
2. Did you take the wrong road? (right)
3. Did he take the early train? (late)
4. Was it an easy test? (very hard)
5. Does she use an expensive camera? (cheap)
6. Did Jenny buy green shoes? (red)
7. Did you have a nice day for the picnic? (rainy)
8. Did they wear long dresses there? (short)
9. Do you prefer British cars? (German)
10. Did she take the clean clothes to the laundry? (dirty)
11. Is your house on a quiet street? (noisy)

C. Study the pictures. Then answer the questions. Use an article, an appropriate adjective, and **one** or **ones**.

1. What kind of day was it?
   A beautiful one, A nice one, etc.
2. What kind of mistake was it?
3. Which shoes are Mr. Gist's?
4. Which suitcase is yours?

55 Modifiers and Substitutes: Ordinals

the **first** page	the **next** person
the **first** (one)	the **next** (one)

A. Study the pictures. Fill in blanks 1–7 with an ordinal modifier (**first**). Fill in blanks 8–14 with a substitute (**first one**). Use ordinal numbers (**first, second,** etc.) or the words **next** and **last**.

We spent a week at the beach. The ___first___ (1) day it was cloudy. The _____(2) day it rained. The _____(3) and _____(4) days were cool. The sun came out on the _____(5) day but it was windy. Finally, on the _____(6) and _____(7) days it turned hot and sunny.

The weather wasn't always good, but I enjoyed myself. I read a book every day. The **first one** (8) was a biography. The _____(9) and _____(10) were science fiction stories. The _____(11) was about diving in the ocean, and the _____(12) and _____(13) were travel books. Then the _____(14) was an American classic, *The Scarlet Letter*.

B. Answer the questions. Use an ordinal number in your answer.

Ex. What day of the week is Tuesday?
   It's the third (day).

1. What month of the year is September?
2. What birthday do you celebrate this year?
3. What's the top floor in the Empire State Building? (102 floors)
4. What day is the next payment due? (May 25)
5. Which president of the U.S. was Abraham Lincoln? (16)
6. What place did your favorite horse finish in? (8)
7. Which unit are we studying now?

56 Modifiers and Substitutes: Demonstratives

This book		These books	
This (one)	is red	These	are interesting.
That book		Those books	
That (one)	is blue	Those	are boring.

A. Fill in the blanks with the modifier **this** or **these** in sentences 1–7. Fill in the blanks with **that** or **those** in 8–14.

1. I like ___this___ necktie, but I don't like ___these___ socks.
2. I bought _____ gloves, but Joe gave me _____ shirt.
3. She made _____ salad, but she didn't make _____ cookies.
4. He'll sell _____ chairs, but he won't sell _____ table.
5. I like _____ job, but I don't like _____ long hours.
6. _____ park is beautiful, but _____ benches are broken.
7. I can fix ___that___ lamp, but I can't fix ___those___ radios.
8. You'll need _____ pillow, but you won't need _____ blankets.
9. I spilled _____ nuts, but I didn't spill _____ sugar.
10. She went back to _____ restaurant, but she didn't find _____ tickets.
11. I don't remember _____ lady, but I remember _____ people.
12. He found _____ books. They were in _____ briefcase.

B. Student 1: ask questions like the model. Use the word **this** or **these**. Student 2: use **that** or **those** in the answer.

> Are these <u>dictionaries</u>?
> No, **those are** <u>dictionaries</u>.

Ex. a duck
Is this a duck? No, that's a duck.

1. the dining room
2. gold rings
3. the receptionist
4. a strong chair
5. good cookies
6. her umbrella
7. new envelopes
8. ice cream
9. your tapes

C. Form another sentence about each picture. Use **this one, that one, these,** or **those**.

1. This barn is new. **That one is old.**
2. These oranges come from Florida.
3. That factory makes shoes.
4. This bus goes to Marin.
5. J. D. Nelson wrote those books.

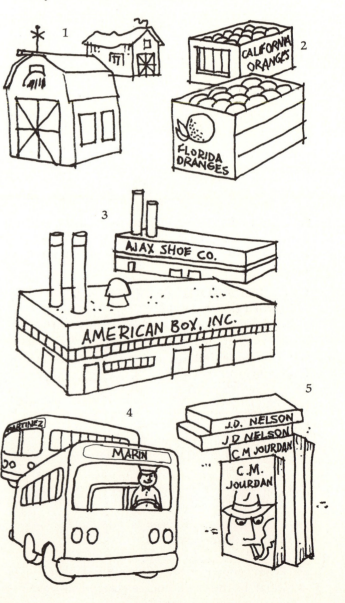

57 Modifiers: other

I want **another** coin.   Get **the other** coin.
I want **other** coins.   Get **the other** coins.

A. Read each sentence. Then form another sentence like the example. Use **the other** and the noun in parentheses.

Ex. Jack is tall. (men)
   The other men are short.
   (or) **The other men aren't tall.**

1. Richmond is close. (city)
2. Ann has short hair. (women)
3. MacArthur Boulevard is noisy. (streets)
4. Henry ate a hot dog. (child)
5. Monday was sunny. (days)
6. *Rocky Road* is an American film. (movie)
7. The apple pie is cheap. (dessert)
8. Sue did well in math. (subjects)
9. We learned a lot from Mrs. Jackson. (teacher)
10. I have $6,000 in this account. (bank)

B. Fill in the blanks with **other** or **another** and a noun from the list.

| doctor | instruments | students | TV set |
| exam | restaurants | sweater | trips |

1. I'm getting cold. I'm putting on **another sweater**.
2. Betty plays the piano. She plays _____ too.
3. They serve water here. You have to ask for water at _____.
4. She likes Puerto Rico. She wants to take _____ there.
5. We all wanted to watch different programs. We got _____.
6. We have a lot of sick people in this town. We need _____.
7. Tom did a report on Canada. _____ did reports on states of the U.S.
8. The teacher tested them the first week. Then they had _____ on the last day of class.

C. Form two sentences about each picture. Use the verb (or verb phrase) in the first sentence. Use **another**, **other**, or **the other** and the noun in the second.

1. rain (verb)//storm
   It will rain on Tuesday.
   We'll have another storm on Thursday.
2. pay the gas//bills
3. visit Mary//friend
4. grow corn//vegetables

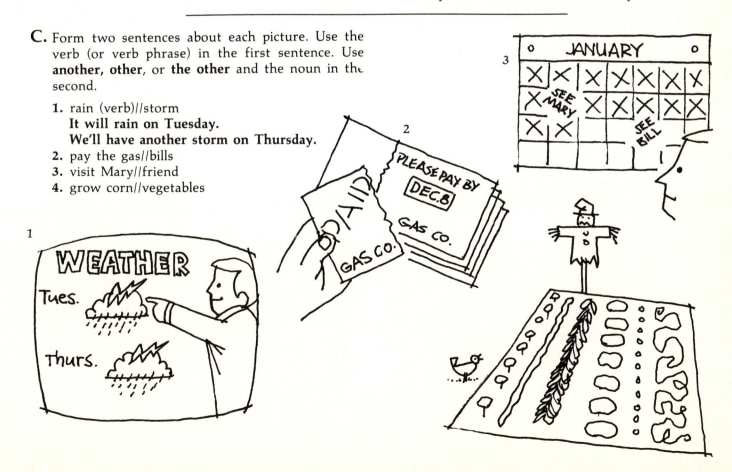

58 Substitutes: other (one)

I want **another (one)**. Get **the other (one)**.
I want **other (one)**s. Get **the other (one)**s.

A. Answer the questions like the examples. Use **the other one** or **the others**.

Ex. A. Are the girls short? (2//1/very tall)
Two are short. The other one is very tall.
Ex. B. Are the students Japanese? (10//2/Indonesian)
Ten are Japanese. The others are Indonesian.

1. Were the speeches long? (1//1/not long)
2. Are the phones in Room 206? (1//4/in Room 210)
3. Are the glasses plastic? (1//5/glass)
4. Are those buildings banks? (1//1/library)
5. Were those men doctors? (1//17/engineers)
6. Do those planes arrive in the morning? (1//1/in the afternoon)
7. Were those cars new? (5//1/very old)
8. Are those students taking English? (5//1/French)
9. Are the stores having sales? (3//2/not having sales)
10. Do those workers live in Albany? (12//1/Emeryville)

B. Fill in the blanks with **another one** or **others**.

1. This apple's bad. I want **another one**.
2. The Cortland apple was good. Now I want three _____.
3. His name is on some lists, and it isn't on _____.
4. Their car was getting old. They got _____.
5. Our suitcase is full. We need _____.
6. They have a car, but they need _____.
7. I like some sports, and I don't like _____.
8. Sometimes people help me, and sometimes I help _____.

C. Form sentences about each picture. Use **another**, **others**, **the other**, or **the others**.

1. bottle/full//empty
   One bottle is full. The others are empty.
2. policeman/fat//thin
3. suitcase/Bob's//Paul's//Robbie's
4. window/open//closed
5. squirrel/climbing//drinking//getting nuts
6. newspaper/from Britain//from Argentina//from Mexico

59 Personal Pronouns: Subject

I	we
you	you
he, she, it	they

A. Ruth and Jim Forbes are spending the evening at the home of Ed and Alice Quick. Fill in the blanks with **I**, **we**, or **you** (singular or plural).

Jim: Ruth and **I** are planning our vacation.
Ed: Oh, great! Where are ____ going?
Ruth: Jim wants to go to the mountains. ____ want to go to the seashore. ____'re just not sure yet.
Jim: Are ____ and Alice taking a vacation this year?
Ed: Oh, yes. ____'re going to the shore.
Alice: To the shore? ____ want to go to the mountains!

B. Match sentences 1–6 with sentences a–f. Fill in the blanks with personal pronouns in a–f. They will refer to the underlined words in 1–6.

1. <u>Dave</u> is out of town now.
2. <u>Diane</u> is an intelligent girl.
3. <u>Linda and her sister</u> are in college.
4. I can't beat <u>Mr. Tammi</u>.
5. I washed <u>my bedroom window</u>.
6. <u>The Wymans</u> bought a house.

a. ____ are studying the same subjects.
b. ____ can lift 350 pounds.
c. **He** is on vacation.
d. ____ paid a lot for it.
e. ____ studies hard and gets good marks.
f. ____ was very dirty.

C. Study the pictures. Then answer the questions. Use a subject pronoun; it will refer to the underlined words.

1. Where's <u>Dave</u>? **He's on vacation.**
   (or) **He's out of town/at the beach.**
2. What's <u>Diane</u> doing?
3. What happened to <u>the painting</u>?
4. "Where are <u>you</u> now, Madeline?"
5. Are <u>Jack and Susan</u> on their way home?
6. What does <u>Mr. Tammi</u> do every day?

60 Personal Pronouns: Object

me	us
you	you
him, her, it	them

A. Student 1: ask questions like the model. Substitute the subject in the question. Student 2: answer the questions. Use the correct object pronoun.

> Is <u>Mr. Thorpe</u> coming?
> Yes, Tom just called **him**.

Ex. You
> **Are you coming?**
> **Yes, Tom just called me.**

1. you and Robert
2. Martha
3. Martha and Gloria
4. the old man
5. Mrs. Thorpe
6. your mother
7. the children
8. the boss
9. I
10. Miss Ford
11. Gloria and I
12. You and I

B. Fill in the blanks with an object pronoun. It will refer to the underlined words.

1. Where's <u>Miss Varney</u>? We need __her__ now.
2. Did you wash <u>this cup</u>? I see some dirt on _____.
3. I forgot the <u>tickets</u>. I left _____ on the table.
4. <u>Robert</u> is very sick. I visited _____ in the hospital Monday.
5. <u>Betty and Marilyn</u> need a ride. I'll take _____.
6. Are <u>Bernice and I</u> invited? They didn't send _____ an invitation.
7. <u>I</u> am going to wash the car. Call _____ later.
8. <u>Bernice</u> was downtown yesterday. I saw _____ in the store.
9. That's <u>my teacher</u>, Mr. Harper. I like _____ very much.
10. <u>Your parrot</u> looks hungry. When did you feed _____?
11. <u>You</u> were there? That's strange. I didn't see _____.
12. <u>We</u> invited the Harpers. Now they're going to invite _____.
13. <u>She</u> was talking very softly. I didn't hear _____.
14. I read a good <u>book</u>, but I don't remember the name of _____.
15. These <u>chairs</u> are wonderful! Where did you buy _____?

C. A friend is visiting you in the hospital. Study the picture. Then answer the questions. Use an object pronoun; it will refer to the underlined words.

Ex. How are they treating <u>you</u>? **They're taking good care of me** (or) **They're treating me fine.**

1. Do you like <u>the nurse</u>?
2. Do you know <u>your roommate</u>?
3. Where did you put <u>the flowers</u>?
4. Where did you put <u>my get-well card</u>?

61 Personal Pronouns: Possessive Modifiers

my	our
your	your
his, her, its	their

A. Form sentences like the model. Substitute the words. Use the correct possessive modifier.

He keeps **his** money there.

Ex. We/car
We keep our car there.

1. I/car
2. She/money
3. They/food
4. Bob and I/shoes
5. Jean and her husband/shoes
6. Robert/clothes
7. Jean/dresses
8. Mr. and Mrs. Case/important papers
9. You and your daughter/good dresses
10. The workers/tools
11. The squirrel/food

B. Match sentences 1–8 with a–h. Fill in the blanks with the correct possessive modifier.

1. Bob and I learned English easily.
2. I'm not going to watch the news.
3. Mr. Hayes took Jim and Bill Hayes to the zoo.
4. Jean needs a new window pane.
5. I'm happy for you and Fred.
6. I'm working in Mrs. Hendrick's house.
7. Oscar was working on the car.
8. You'll get cold.

a. He's _____ grandfather.
b. _____ hands are all dirty.
c. I'm painting _____ kitchen.
d. She measured _____ height and width.
e. _____ TV set isn't working.
f. **Our** American friends spoke it all the time.
g. I like _____ new house.
h. You need _____ coat.

C. Study the pictures. Then answer the questions. Use a possessive modifier.

1. What's he taking off?
   He's taking off his shoes.
   What will he do with the towel?
   He'll dry his feet.
2. What's she warming?
   How is the man getting warm?
3. What is the clock missing?
   What's the matter with the book?
4. What did the woman forget?
   What will the man do?

62 Personal Pronouns: Possessive

mine	ours
yours	yours
his, hers	theirs

A. Student 1: Form two sentences like the model. Student 2: Form a third sentence like the model. Use the correct possessive pronoun.

Don didn't buy the pin. Anna did.
Then it's **hers**.

Ex. Anna/ring//I
Anna didn't buy the ring. I did. Then it's yours

1. I/picture//you
2. You/book//the employees
3. The company/record//Hugo
4. Hugo/hammer//Mr. Sibley
5. Mr. Sibley/mirror//his wife
6. Mrs. Sibley/radio//you and I
7. You and I/piano//the Sibleys
8. You and Hugo/camera//Don and I
9. Don and I/vase//our friend
10. Our friend/cake//we

B. Fill in the blanks with the correct possessive pronoun.

1. He can't eat that soup. It's not ___his___.
2. We don't own the house, but the furniture is _____.
3. John has a lot of shoes. Those slippers are _____ too.
4. That suitcase belongs to John and me. The jeep is _____ too.
5. This isn't my raincoat. I'll ask that woman. It's probably _____.
6. That isn't my watch. _____ is gold.
7. This isn't the Shacklefords' car. _____ has a black roof.
8. This isn't our room. _____ is Number 401.
9. I have to borrow a dictionary. I didn't bring _____.
10. This book doesn't belong to Mary. _____ is over there.
11. Bill's working at a desk, but it isn't _____.
12. Joan and Bill wrote letters. I answered hers. Now I'll answer _____.

C. Study the pictures. Then fill in the blanks with a possessive pronoun.

1. "Her dress is like _____."
2. "This shirt isn't _____."
3. "These keys are _____."
4. "Our children aren't in your pool. _____ are swimming in _____."

63 Personal Pronouns: Reflexive

myself	ourselves
yourself	yourselves
himself, herself, itself	themselves

A. Form sentences like the model. Substitute the subject. Use the correct reflexive pronoun as object.

> She almost burned **herself**.

Ex. He
He almost burned himself.

1. We
2. They
3. You
4. I
5. Gary and Ellen
6. You and Ken
7. Mrs. Cunningham
8. The waitress
9. Her brother
10. Barry and I
11. The cat
12. Some people

B. Fill in the blanks with a reflexive pronoun.

1. Ken opened the can by <u>himself</u>.
2. The teachers typed the exams by _____.
3. Some artists get a lot of paint on _____.
4. The engine just stopped by _____.
5. We changed the tire by _____.
6. John got some cake for _____.
7. That old man is always talking to _____.
8. Ellen pulled the blanket over _____.
9. She's lonely. She often has to eat by _____.
10. I sold some coins, but I kept the valuable ones for _____.
11. Children can walk by _____ at one year old.
12. I'll give you the pencil, but I need the pen for _____.
13. Barry sleeps upstairs by _____.
14. You're not being fair to _____.
15. That record player turns off by _____.

C. Form a sentence about each picture. Use a verb from the list and a reflexive pronoun.

buy cut see surprise

1. **That boy is cutting himself.**
   (or) **He cut himself badly.**

64 Personal Pronouns: Summary

I   me   my   mine   myself

A. Complete the sentences. Use **and** and change the subject and object pronouns.

1. She hit him, **and he hit her.**
2. He likes her, _____.
3. They remember me, _____.
4. I believed him, _____.
5. She's helping us, _____.
6. You need me, _____.
7. It's touching you, _____.
8. We wanted them, _____.

B. Fill in the blanks with a personal pronoun. It will refer to the underlined words.

1. Ann's driving Floyd's car, and he's driving **hers**.
2. The Frakes washed their car, and the Fords washed _____.
3. Our son is one year old. _____ walks by _____ now.
4. My suitcase was very heavy. The bus driver helped _____.

5. My uncle burned _____ arm with hot water.
6. The cat caught _____ tail in the door.
7. The children are quiet upstairs. _____ are in bed.
8. Jan left _____ office a few minutes ago.
9. Tomorrow is Jan's birthday. Herb's buying a gift for _____.
10. Mrs. Preble made sandwiches for the children. _____ didn't make one for _____.
11. This seat isn't that lady's; _____ is over there.
12. I can't use this hand. I burned _____ last week.
13. Mr. Kidd broke _____ arm. _____ can't dress _____ now.
14. Your hair looks good, but I can't fix _____ like that.
15. I was talking to the barber. The next customer was listening to _____.
16. You and your sister are all dirty. Wash _____ well and come to dinner.

C. Fill in the blanks with a personal pronoun.

Ted: Hurry up! **You'll** be late for the dance.
Joe: _____ can't find _____ tie! Can _____ borrow one of _____?
Ted: Yes, here's _____ best red one.
Joe: Hey, that isn't _____ tie. This is one of _____!
Ted: Okay, Okay. Now hurry up!
Joe: All right. _____'m ready now.
Ted: Yeah? Go look at _____ in the mirror.

65 Quantifiers: some, any

I put **some** sugar in my tea.
I didn't put **any** milk in it.

A. Form sentences like the model. Substitute the nouns.

We need some <u>salt</u>, but we don't need any <u>pepper</u>.

Ex. sugar/flour
We need some sugar, but we don't need any flour.

1. cotton/wool
2. apples/lemons
3. soap/toothpaste
4. envelopes/stamps
5. potatoes/rice
6. gas/oil
7. cups/glasses
8. tea/coffee
9. blue pens/red pens
10. clerks/nurses
11. water/food

B. Student 1: ask a question like the examples. Use either **some** or **any**. Student 2: answer each question.

Ex. A. dessert//Yes
Do you want any dessert?
Yes, please I'd like some.
Ex. B. grapes//No
Do you want some grapes?
No thanks. I don't want any.

1. pie//No
2. salad//Yes
3. bread//No
4. peaches//Yes
5. beans//No
6. butter//Yes
7. oranges//Yes
8. salt//No
9. water//No
10. nuts//Yes
11. fish//Yes
12. cherries//No

C. Study the pictures. Student 1: fill in the blanks with **some** or **any**. Student 2: answer the question with **some** or **any**.

1. Did <u>any</u> cans fall down?
   Yes, some fell down.
2. Did _____ rice get on the floor?
3. Did he leave _____ apples for you?
4. Did Miss Tutt type _____ letters?
5. Did Barbara eat _____ cookies?
6. Did _____ boys talk to Maxine?

66 Quantifiers: some, any vs. a/an, one

some milk (some)   a cup, an egg (one)
any milk (any)

A. Form sentences like the model. Substitute the noun. Use **some**, **a**, or **an**.

   She bought **some** socks.

   Ex. hat
   She bought a hat.

1. perfume
2. jacket
3. magazines
4. orange juice
5. umbrella
6. toothpaste
7. hairbrush
8. paper cups
9. alarm clock
10. writing paper
11. ticket
12. birthday cards

B. Fill in the blanks with **some**, **any**, **a/an**, or **one**.

1. I'm not saving money for ___a___ car.
2. The customer's waiting for _____ food.
3. Mark didn't drink _____ coffee.
4. We took _____ early train this morning.
5. _____ picture fell off the wall.
6. _____ buttons fell off his shirt.
7. _____ juice got on the floor.
8. They didn't let _____ boys on the team.
9. Mr. Shapiro won't give _____ test today. He gave _____ yesterday.
10. We need _____ fruit. I'll get _____ today.
11. I went for _____ envelopes, but I didn't see _____.
12. I saw _____ elephant once. They have _____ in the zoo.
13. He ordered _____ ice cream but didn't eat _____.
14. She looked for _____ new spring hat but didn't find _____.
15. I got _____ glasses for the juice, but we didn't use _____.
16. I didn't bring _____ napkins, but we needed _____.

C. Study the pictures. Then answer the questions. Use **some** or **any** as modifiers.

1. What did he spill? milk/soup
   He spilled some soup, but he didn't spill any milk.
2. What did she buy? chicken/fish
3. What did John have? dimes/quarters
4. What did Mr. Reed order? paper/tape
5. What did they plant? flowers/vegetables
6. What did he put on his potatoes? pepper/salt

67 Quantifiers: many, much

many sandwiches
much food

A. Form sentences like the model. Substitute the noun. Use **many** or **much**.

I don't have **many** pens.

Ex. time
I don't have much time.

1. money
2. pennies
3. books
4. bread
5. vegetables
6. water
7. ice cream
8. shirts
9. clothes
10. furniture
11. chairs
12. rice

B. Student 1: ask questions like the example.
Student 2: use **many** or **much** in the answer.

Ex. drink/coffee
Do you drink coffee? Yes, but not much.

1. read/books
2. see/movies
3. save/money
4. use/red ink
5. have/time
6. eat/black bread
7. have/American friends
8. buy/records
9. know/American history
10. make/phone calls
11. send/birthday cards
12. play/chess

C. Form a sentence about each picture. Use the verbs and **many** or **much**.

1. (take)
   They didn't take many suitcases.
2. (bake)
3. (grow)
4. (own)
5. (wash)
6. (use)

68 Quantifiers: many, much vs. a lot of

She ate { **a lot of** bread. / **a lot of** beans. / **a lot**. }   I didn't eat { **much** (bread). / **many** (beans). }

A. Form sentences about the picture like the example. Substitute the noun. Use **a lot of** in affirmative sentences and **many** or **much** in negative sentences.

Ex. potatoes
She didn't buy many potatoes.

1. milk
2. fruit
3. corn
4. cookies
5. sugar
6. hot dogs
7. toothpaste
8. light bulbs
9. paper napkins
10. soap

B. Fill in the blanks with **many, much, a lot,** or **a lot of**.

1. Jim's wife spends __a lot of__ money on clothes.
2. She handles _____ phone calls every day.
3. We didn't have _____ rain this afternoon.
4. They don't have _____ street lights on this street.
5. He gave _____ hay to the cows and horses.
6. I hear _____ noise upstairs.
7. Do you save _____ money every week?
8. Did you see _____ shirts on sale?
9. Did she look in _____ stores for the right dress?
10. I don't wear jewelry, but she wears _____.
11. We were in the store a long time, but we didn't buy _____.
12. That zoo has some monkeys, but it doesn't have _____.
13. The kids got wet. _____ changed into dry clothes right away.
14. That boy has a lot of toys. He got _____ from his brother.
15. The lights went out at the dance. The people couldn't see, and _____ left.

69 Quantifiers: a few, a little

a few sandwiches
a little food

A. Form sentences like the model. Substitute the noun. Use **a few** or **a little**.

She needs **a little** money.

Ex. dollars
She needs a few dollars.

1. butter
2. eggs
3. advice
4. handkerchiefs
5. gas
6. bottles
7. medicine
8. red pens
9. change
10. time off
11. help
12. helpers

B. Form sentences like the example. Use **a few** or **a little** in short answers.

Ex. Did any soup spill?
A little did.

1. Did any beans spill?
2. Did any paper burn?
3. Do those students know English?
4. Does smoke get in the rug?
5. Did the people get well fast?
6. Do any Canadians live here?
7. Did any workers leave early on Friday?
8. Are the children sleeping?
9. Is any wood rotten?
10. Were the customers angry?
11. Was that bread dry?
12. Were any bananas ripe?

C. Student 1: ask questions about each picture. Student 2: answer each question. Use **a few** or **a little**.

1. did/eat **What did she eat?**
   She ate a little cheese.
   (or) **She ate a few grapes**, etc.
2. is/ordering
3. did/use
4. will/take on the trip

70 Quantifiers: few, little, no, none

few trees   no trees (none)
little grass   no grass (none)

A. Fill in the blanks with **few** or **little**.

1. Myrtle is on a diet. She eats very __little__ bread.
2. They give a lot to the children's hospital. They give very _____ money to the church.
3. The dance wasn't very good. _____ people came.
4. Mrs. Dickie comes from Michigan. She has _____ relatives in Dallas.
5. I don't like sweet things. I put very _____ jelly on my toast.
6. Mrs. Burnham is just painting one door. She needs very _____ paint.
7. Our bank probably isn't open yet. _____ banks open at 8:00 a.m.
8. We get our vegetables from Texas. _____ vegetables come from New Jersey.
9. That's a men's sickness. _____ women get it.
10. I have a 1970 car. _____ 1970 cars are still running.
11. Her husband doesn't like greens. She puts very _____ lettuce in the salads.
12. This is a new kind of computer. _____ offices have it yet.

B. Form sentences like the examples. Use **no** instead of **not any**. Use **few** or **little** for **not many** or **not much**.

Ex. A. She doesn't make many cookies.
She makes few cookies.
Ex. B. We don't buy any beef.
We buy no beef.

1. We're not getting very many vegetables.
2. We're not getting much rain.
3. He doesn't forget many names.
4. That school doesn't have very many Latin American students.
5. That teacher doesn't give any tests.
6. Not much water spilled on the floor.
7. He doesn't have any money.
8. Not much cold air got into the room.

C. Study the pictures. Fill in the blanks with a noun and **few**, **little**, or **none**.

1. Mr. Nelson looked for __ducks__ but found __few__.
2. I wanted some _____, but they had _____.
3. Many _____ started the race, but _____ finished.
4. J.D. used a lot of _____. Now there's very _____ left.
5. Dr. Li looked for _____, but there was _____ on the shelf.
6. I reached in the bag for _____, but _____ were there.

71 Quantifiers Before Other Modifiers

one of my legs
a little of the time
many of those countries

A. Form sentences like the model. Substitute the quantifier (**one, some,** etc.) or the definite modifier (**the, his,** etc.) Do 1–12 in order.

She borrowed <u>one</u> of <u>the</u> keys.

Ex. some
She borrowed some of the keys.

1. your
2. these
3. three
4. a few
5. my
6. those
7. many
8. the
9. few
10. a lot
11. a couple
12. none

B. Study the pictures. Then complete the sentences.

1. He spilled **some of his water.**
   (or) **He spilled some of the water.**
2. She's picking up _____.
3. I broke _____.
4. He's eating _____.
5. She's eating _____.
6. She can't find _____.
7. He washed _____.

C. Fill in the blanks with a word in parentheses and **of**.

1. The tree lost <u>some of</u> its leaves. (any, some)
2. Henry got _____ the hard jobs. (no, none)
3. I brought _____ my kites. (a, one)
4. Kobayashi didn't know _____ the answers. (any, some)
5. I want _____ those red balloons. (a few, a little)
6. Nancy saw _____ her friends at the party. (few, little)
7. He didn't drink _____ the grape juice. (many, much)
8. They looked for him in _____ those cities. (any, one)
9. They burned _____ the old wood. (a little, five)
10. I can't eat _____ this rice. (many, much)
11. _____ her paper was dirty. (A few, A little)
12. _____ the socks has a hole. (One, Some)

72 Quantifiers: both, all, each, every

both feet	**each** foot
all toes	**every** toe

A. Fill in the blanks with **both, all, each,** or **every**.

1. Sixty people parked in the lot. __All__ the cars were small.
2. We were away last Thursday and Friday. _____ days were rainy.
3. I'm studying about birds. _____ birds have feathers.
4. Walter's carrying a package in _____ hand.
5. They stayed at the beach a week. _____ day was nice.
6. They gave a new shirt to _____ the players on the soccer team.
7. He got $5,000 from his uncle. Now _____ that money is gone.
8. _____ child likes the circus. _____ parents like it too.
9. _____ countries have flags. _____ flag has a story.
10. The doctor checked _____ eye. _____ eyes were bad.

B. Student 1: read the sentence. Student 2: form a yes/no question like the example. Use **of** in the question. Student 1: then give a short answer.

Ex. I burned my fingers. (burn/all)
Did you burn all of them?
Yes, I did.

1. She broke her skis. (break/both)
2. John got fourteen books from the library. (read/all)
3. Maxwell took two tests yesterday. (pass/both)
4. Charles buys gifts for Beatrice and Donna. (like/both)
5. We grew these vegetables in our garden. (grow/all)
6. He remembered his two friends. (give a souvenir/each)
7. Peterson wrote the prices on the boxes. (mark/every one)
8. I have two clocks. (run well/each)
9. The fire caught the small animals. (die/every one)

C. Study the picture. Fill in the blanks with **both, all, each,** or **every**. Use **of** where necessary.

1. The windows are __both__ open.
2. The lights are _____ on.
3. _____ boy has a necktie.
4. _____ the girls are wearing jeans.
5. The boys are hungry; _____ are eating cake.
6. Several girls are talking to _____ boy.
7. One girl is carrying records. She'll listen to _____ them tonight.
8. The young people will dance to these records. _____ has dance music on it.

73 Quantifiers: half, quarter, etc.

(a) **half** (of) the pieces
a third of the water
three-quarters of the building

A. Study the table. Student 1: form questions like the example about the Smiths' family expenses. Use **half of, a quarter of**, etc. Student 2: give the correct information in the answer.

Ex. half/the house payment
Do they spend half of their money on the house payment? No, (only) a quarter of it.

1. a quarter/taxes and insurance
2. half/utilities and repairs
3. a quarter/food
4. a sixteenth/medical expenses
5. an eighth/the car and bus
6. a quarter/entertainment
7. an eighth/clothes and miscellaneous

B. Fill in the blanks with a quantifier: **a tenth, two-fifths**, etc.

I'm reading a new book about Florida. It tells many things about the state. <u>A tenth</u> (1) of the book is about geography. Another _____(2) is about its history. The chapter on government takes up _____(3) of the book, and the one on cultures occupies another _____(4). _____(5) of the pages deal with Florida's economy. A short chapter, only _____(6) of the book, is about sports. The last _____(7) discusses the state's future.

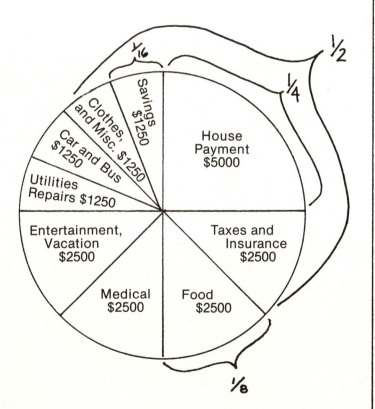

CONTENTS

CHAPTERS	PAGES	
1. Natural Geography	1 - 50	(1/10)
2. History	51 -200	(3/10)
3. Government	201-250	(1/10)
4. Economy	251-350	(1/5)
5. Cultures	351-400	(1/10)
6. Sports	400-425	(1/20)
7. The Future	426-500	(3/20)

74 Summary of Articles and Other Modifiers

See summary table of modifiers
in the Appendix

A. Form sentences like the model. Substitute the modifier. Use the uncountable noun **bread** or the countable noun **cookie**. Sometimes you can use either.

My roommate ate his **bread**.

Ex. A. some
My roommate ate some bread.
(or) **My roommate ate some cookies.**
Ex. B. a
My roommate ate a cookie.

1. every
2. those
3. a little
4. that
5. another
6. a few
7. both
8. the other
9. many
10. my
11. each
12. the last

B. Fill in the blanks with the modifiers in parentheses.

1. I'm looking for __a__ hat. I'll buy __that__ big one. (a, that)
2. She's hungry for _____ meat. She'll eat _____ ham. (a little, this)
3. She bought _____ coats. One has _____ soft collar. (a, both)
4. He caught _____ fish in _____ lake. (many, the)
5. _____ car is _____ Ford. (a, my)
6. We don't have _____ tomatoes. We ate _____ tomatoes. (any, the)
7. _____ children are playing over there. _____ voices are loud. (some, their)
8. They wrote _____ letter to me. _____ letter came yesterday. (a, the)
9. She put on _____ socks. _____ feet were cold. (her, some)

C. Fill in the blanks with a quantifier. Form more sentences about the picture.

The store has **a lot of** eggs. It doesn't have _____ butter. Mr. Ladd is taking _____ quarts of milk. He has _____ bread in his cart, but he has _____ sweet things.

75 Summary of Pronouns and Other Substitutes

See summary table of substitutes in the Appendix

A. Fill in the blanks with a substitute word from the parentheses.

1. This one is mine. **That one** is yours. (That one, It)
2. This telephone is busy. _____ is out of order. (The other one, All)
3. Do you have time to talk to me? Yes, I have _____. (a little, little)
4. That theater had three good movies this summer. I saw _____. (every, every one)
5. Four friends went to the soccer game. _____ bought his own ticket. (Every, Each)
6. That was a good sandwich. I think I'll have _____. (another, every)
7. Did Ted have any friends in high school? Yes, he had _____. (few, a few)
8. John was lost in the forest. He had nothing to eat and _____ to drink. (little, none)
9. Do we have any eggs for breakfast? No, we have _____. (none, a few)
10. We bought a quart of chocolate ice cream. Do you want _____? (some, little)
11. This knife isn't sharp. Where's _____? (another one, a few)
12. Tomato soup was three cans for a dollar. _____ costs thirty cents. (Each, Every)
13. I like Tom and I also like his wife Mary. _____ are my very close friends. (Both, All)
14. A lot of people were invited to the party, but _____ came. (a few, few)
15. Don doesn't drink much wine, but he feels _____ doesn't hurt him. (a little, little)

B. Study the picture. Read the sentence about Ted. Form another sentence about Phil. Use a pronoun substitute.

1. Ted is in one bed.
   Phil's in the other.
2. Ted broke one leg.
3. Ted's bed has many pillows.
4. Ted has a tall nurse.
5. Ted got few flowers.
6. Ted got many get-well cards.
7. Ted takes a lot of medicine.
8. Ted reads one or two magazines.
9. Ted wants this program on TV.

76 Compound Noun Phrases with *and*

you **and** I
Dick **and** Janice
a big one **and** a little one

A. Form sentences like the model. Substitute the noun phrases.

<u>I</u> saw <u>some deer</u> in <u>the woods</u>.

Ex. Dick and I/a dog/the garage
Dick and I saw a dog in the garage.

1. Dick and Janice/a play/London
2. The first child and the second one/an airplane/the sky
3. We and our neighbors/an accident/our neighborhood
4. She/strange fruit and vegetables/the store
5. A neighbor/you and Janice/the park
6. Dick/a play and a movie/Paris
7. The tourists/plays/London and Paris
8. She/birds/the big tree and the little one
9. We/water on the floor/the bathroom and the kitchen
10. John and Jim/a mouse/the living room

B. Fill in the blanks with a compound noun phrase. Use the nouns in the list. Also use **a** and **the** where necessary.

buses/trucks   dimes/nickels
carpenter/electrician I/Mr. Spencer
cereal/fruit   magazine/newspaper
city/country   paper/pens
coat/sweater

1. He ate **cereal and fruit** for breakfast.
2. Miss Preble had only _____ in her purse.
3. The kids need _____ for their drawing.
4. We'll call _____. They'll fix it.
5. They have houses in _____.
6. _____ weren't at the party.
7. I'm going to wear _____ today.
8. She read about it in _____.
9. _____ don't use that road.

C. Study the picture. Answer the questions. Use compound noun phrases.

1. What's on the wall of the office?
   A picture and a calendar.
2. What's on Jan's desk?
3. What's she wearing today?
4. What does she use water for?
5. What's in the waste basket?
6. What does she keep in the top drawer?

77 Compound Noun Phrases with or

cake **or** doughnuts
Mary **or** Sidney
a big dish **or** a little one

A. Form sentences like the model. Substitute the noun phrases in the **or** compound.

   Did Mary tell <u>you</u> or <u>Mr. Lamb</u>?

Ex. her friend/Mr. Lamb
   Did Mary tell her friend or Mr. Lamb?

1. her friend/Bill
2. the librarian/Bill
3. the librarian/a relative
4. the children/a relative
5. the children/the neighbors
6. Mrs. Sash/Mr. Sash
7. the secretary/her boss
8. you/your brother
9. your brother/her brother
10. the first man/the second one

B. Student 1: complete each question with **or** and a noun from the list. Student 2: answer with one of the nouns.

| bank | girl's name | hot one | lawyers | passenger |
| furniture | hamburger | jelly | magazine | pants |

1. Do you want a hot dog <u>**or a hamburger**</u>?
   A hot dog please. (or) **A hamburger.**
2. Is she reading a newspaper _____?
3. Is she wearing a skirt _____?
4. Is Sidney a boy's name _____?
5. Will tomorrow be a warm day _____?
6. Do they sell rugs _____ in that store?
7. Is the library _____ closed today?
8. Is cheese _____ good on this bread?
9. Did the bus driver _____ get mad first?
10. Do farmers _____ like that law?

C. Student 1: form questions about the picture. Use **or**.
Student 2: answer with a full sentence.

1. table/bench
   Are the flowers on a table or a bench?
   They're on a table.
2. knives/scissors
3. vase/lamp
4. skirts/pants
5. day/night
6. picture of a house/picture of a barn

SECTION THREE

78 Sentences with be and Complement

Is that	**a bee?**	[noun]
The bees **aren't**	**inside** (the house).	[adverb]
I am	**glad.**	[adjective]

A. Form sentences like the model. Substitute the subject or the complement. Use **am, are,** or **is.** Do 1–12 in order.

<u>The umbrella **is** wet.</u>

Ex. Your shoes
Your shoes are wet.

1. in the closet
2. A mouse
3. a quiet animal
4. That cat
5. lazy
6. I
7. on the phone
8. She
9. the new manager
10. forty years old
11. The houses
12. near the road

B. Form three sentences about subjects 1–8. Use any tense form of **be** and complements: a noun, an adverb, and an adjective.

	Nouns	**Adverbs**	**Adjectives**
1. A crow	a. a bird	i. at the door	q. big
2. A hammer	b. a tool	j. in the sink	r. black
3. Her birthday party	c. a lot of fun	k. last Friday	s. broken
4. His English test	d. a quiet place	l. near the bank	t. clever
5. Jack	e. an easy one	m. on the bench	u. heavy
6. The cups	f. Mr. Kessler	n. on the roof	v. lost
7. The library	g. plastic	o. outside	w. old
8. The new teacher	h. the best player	p. tomorrow	x. very easy

1. **A crow is a bird. A crow is on the roof. A crow is black.**

C. Student 1: ask yes/no questions about the picture. Use the past, present, or future of **be.** Student 2: give a short answer.

Ex. funny/that book
Is that book funny?
Yes, it is.

1. big/the ball
2. on a tricycle/the child
3. angry/the lady
4. her dress/wet
5. on the bench/the glass
6. the flowers/by the house
7. on/the lady's shoes

79 Sentences with Linking Verb and Complement

    Do I   look well?
    You (don't) look well.

A. Student 1: ask a yes/no question like the model. Substitute a verb or complement. Student 2: give a short **no** answer. Then give an affirmative statement. Do 1–12 in order.

  Does it <u>look good</u>? No, it doesn't. It <u>looks bad</u>.

Ex. red//brown
  Does it look red? No, it doesn't. It looks brown.

1. turn
2. strong//weak
3. taste
4. awful//great
5. feel
6. terrible//nice
7. sound
8. old//new
9. seem
10. taste like coffee//tea
11. smell like
12. fish//meat

B. Form an affirmative and a negative sentence about each subject 1–8. Use a linking verb a–h and complement i–p.

1. His test
2. That noise
3. The air
4. The flowers
5. The meeting
6. The room
7. These apples
8. Your friend

a. feel/feels
b. is/are becoming
c. looked
d. smell/smells
e. sounded
f. was/were getting
g. will seem
h. will taste

i. a problem//a help
j. beautiful//ugly
k. cold//hot
l. easy//very hard
m. like a cow//like a pig
n. long//short
o. sweet//sour
p. terrible//good

1. His test will seem easy. It won't seem very hard.

C. Form affirmative and negative sentences about the picture. Use linking verbs and a complement from the list.

    busy   expensive
    crowded   fresh
    dirty   noisy
    excited   soft

Ex. The street **looks crowded.**

1. The shops _____.
2. The tourists _____.
3. The children _____.
4. The fruit _____.
5. The wooden plates _____.
6. The cloth _____.
7. The animals _____.

80 Sentences with Verb and Direct Object

> Is he learning **German?**
> He is('s) learning **English.**
> He isn't learning **German.**

A. Student 1: ask a yes/no question like the example. Use present tense in 1–3, past tense in 4–7, and future in 8–11. Student 2: give a short **no** answer. Then give an affirmative statement.

Ex. rabbits/eat meat//eat vegetables
Do rabbits eat meat? No, they don't. They eat vegetables.

1. that bottle/hold a gallon//hold two quarts
2. a fish/have feet//have fins
3. Mr. Potter/draw pictures//draw maps
4. the boss/use a pencil//use a pen
5. Johnny/drink coffee//drink milk
6. Lily/write a story//write a poem
7. the Yankees/lose the first game//lose the second game
8. the airplane/bring food//bring blankets
9. Mrs. Drop/visit France//visit Scotland
10. Rudy/fight Max//fight Sal
11. you/call the Maidwell Company//call the Byrite Company

B. Complete the sentences like the example. Put the words in parentheses in the correct order.

Ex. She _____. (arithmetic/is/teaching)
She is teaching arithmetic.

1. The soccer ball _____. (one player's arm/touched)
2. Fred _____. (burn/doesn't/his old newspapers)
3. The sickness _____. (in the city/killed/many rats)
4. His wife _____. (moved/the sofa/to the other side)
5. I _____. (don't/English/understand/well)
6. We _____. (about $50/at the restaurant/spend/will)
7. They _____. (allow/dogs/don't/inside)

C. Form sentences about each picture. Use the verbs in the past tense and a direct object.

cook//eat   cross//enter   open//drink   sell//buy

1. **They cooked a fish. Then they ate it.**

81 Sentences with No Direct Objects

> Did she **walk?**
> She **ran.**
> She didn't **walk.**

A. Student 1: ask a yes/no question like the example. Use present tense in 1–3, past tense in 4–7, and future in 8–11. Student 2: give a short **no** answer. Then give an affirmative statement.

Ex. the baby/cry//play
Does the baby cry? No, she doesn't. She plays.

1. a dog/moo//bark
2. a penguin/fly//swim
3. the sun/rise in the west//rise in the east
4. Mr. Ramsay/write//call
5. Rita/pass//fail
6. the farmer/walk//drive
7. the horses/run out//stay inside
8. Miss Ventola/sing//dance
9. John/remember//forget
10. the Tigers/lose//win
11. those people/leave early//stay late

B. Form sentences like the example. Put the words in the correct order.

Ex. begin/didn't/during the night/the rain
The rain didn't begin during the night.

1. Florence/loudly/speaks
2. doesn't/my brother/understand
3. fast/learn/some people
4. are/leaving/now/the Greens
5. are going to/on Tuesday/they/vote
6. Al/drive/to the airport/will
7. don't/in St. Louis/play/the Giants

C. Form sentences about each picture. Use the verbs in the past tense.

fall//break   run//escape
work//play   change//stop

1. A lamp fell. It broke.

82 Sentences with Indirect Objects

I gave **Judy** some money.
She got **me** a sandwich.

A. Form sentences like example. Add the indirect object in parentheses.

Ex. Mr. Smith write a letter. (the company)
Mr. Smith wrote the company a letter.

1. Mrs. Jones bought a new shirt. (her husband)
2. Mr. Brown is paying a hundred dollars. (Mr. Green)
3. Miss Johnson is showing the spring coats. (a customer)
4. Mr. Williams doesn't lend money. (people)
5. Mrs. Miller gives advice. (students)
6. I read a story every night. (my son)
7. Diane is teaching English in the living room. (Pedro)
8. Our teacher didn't tell the answer right away. (us)
9. They were sending messages in Spanish. (him)
10. Joe wants to get a bracelet. (Donna)
11. Joy is going to make a bowl of soup. (Dave)

B. What did Christine buy? Form six sentences like the example.

Ex. Christine got **her mother a wallet** for Christmas.

C. Complete the sentences like the example. Put the words in parentheses in the correct order.

Ex. The company . . . (now/owes/$34/you)
The company now owes you $34.

1. We ____. (last year/600 boxes/sold/them)
2. I ____. (a seat/didn't find/in that row/us)
3. Gina ____. (a gift/him/isn't giving/on his birthday)
4. Michele ____. (a hard question/asked/her father/yesterday)
5. Eric ____. (a birthday card/his mother/last night/was making)
6. A policeman ____. (gave/on Grand Avenue/some people/tickets)
7. Mrs. Simpson ____. (a pie/her family/in the kitchen/is baking)

83 Sentences with to or for + Indirect Object

Did he give a pin **to you**?
I will get a ticket **for you**.

A. Fill in the blanks with an object pronoun and **to** or **for** with an indirect object.

1. Miss Butterfield has a ticket. Josh **got it for her**. (get)
2. I have my keys again. Betty _____. (find)
3. Paul has a new camera. His father _____. (buy)
4. We ordered some shirts. The company _____. (send)
5. Ted and Don know the Greek alphabet. Mr. Lipson _____. (teach)
6. Sarah is playing with Bill's toys. I _____. (give)
7. John received a card from Mary. She _____. (make)
8. His wife needed a towel. He _____. (bring)
9. I heard that story. My sister _____. (tell)
10. Birds eat pieces of bread. We _____. (leave)
11. Bob and I wanted Mr. Sheldon's kites. He _____. (sell)
12. You'll need Mrs. Cutter's scissors. She _____. (lend)

B. Answer the questions like the example. Answer **no** and a full sentence. Use **to** or **for** in the answer.

Ex. Did John give Mary that pin? (Fred)
No, Fred gave it to her.

1. Did John owe Penny $45? (Fred)
2. Did John give you these socks? (Emily)
3. Did Emily leave you this umbrella? (Walter)
4. Does Walter make the children toys? (I)
5. Is Dick's mother reading him the story? (his sister)
6. Was Emily writing Dick a letter? (his grandmother)
7. Were Dick and Jane getting the teacher a gift? (Tony and Marie)
8. Will Mr. Burton show Carol and Bob the house? (Mr. Cook)
9. Is Nelson going to bring me the paper? (Carol)

C. Form one or more sentences about each picture. Use verbs from Parts A and B and **to** or **for** with an indirect object.

1. **That woman is making a pie for her family.** (or) **She's going to give a pie to the children.**

84 Sentences with be vs. do Verbs

Joni **is** a blonde.   She **isn't** a brunette.
Joni **has** blonde hair.   She **doesn't have** black hair.

A. Fill in the blanks with the correct negative from the parentheses.

1. The Ortegas __aren't__ Mexicans. (aren't, don't)
2. This telephone _____ work. (doesn't, isn't)
3. The driver _____ remember me. (didn't, wasn't)
4. Her birthday _____ tomorrow. (doesn't, isn't)
5. A triangle _____ have four sides. (doesn't, isn't)
6. Trees _____ grow well there. (aren't, don't)
7. The cows _____ in the field. (didn't, weren't)
8. My leg _____ hurt now. (doesn't, isn't)
9. Cindy _____ fat now. (doesn't, isn't)
10. Your gloves _____ the right color. (aren't, don't)
11. The sun _____ shine all day. (didn't, wasn't)
12. Mr. Snyder _____ the boss. (didn't, wasn't)

B. Form affirmative and negative sentences like the example. Use the present tense of **be** or one of the verbs on this list:

carry	eat	read	wear
drive	have	sell	write

Ex. The subway/passengers//freight
The subway carries passengers.
It doesn't carry freight.

1. A penguin/a bird//a fish
2. Clara Norris/books//music
3. Rabbits/vegetables//meat
4. My car/a Ford//a Volkswagen
5. I/a Ford//a Volkswagen
6. Those books/dictionaries//textbooks
7. Jenny/magazines//the newspaper
8. Jerry/a heavy sweater//a coat
9. I/fruit//candy
10. Mr. Ortega/a Peruvian//a Mexican
11. He/insurance//houses

C. Student 1: ask a yes/no question about each picture. Use the verbs **be** or **do**. Student 2: give a short **yes** or **no** answer.

1. **Does the nest have eggs? Yes, it does.**
   (or) **Is the bird in the nest? No, it isn't.**

85 There sentences: Affirmative and Negative

There is/There's a table in the yard.
There aren't any chairs.

A. Form sentences like the model. Substitute the subject, the form of **be**, and or the complement. Use the correct singular or plural form of **be**. Do 1–12 in order.

There is sugar on the cake.

Ex. candles
There are candles on the cake.

1. were
2. a big candle
3. in the box
4. is
5. will be
6. on the table
7. gifts
8. for the children
9. are going to be
10. a party
11. on your birthday
12. a surprise

B. Student 1: fill in the blanks with the first group of words in parentheses. Student 2: respond. Use the second group of words.

1. There are _____ in the soup. (some carrots//peas)
   There are some carrots in the soup.
   I know, but there aren't any peas in the soup
2. There were _____ at the party. (some Japanese//Greeks)
3. There are _____ on the American flag. (stars//letters)
4. There'll be _____ in February. (a furniture sale//a book sale)
5. There's going to be _____ tomorrow. (an English test//a science test)
6. There are _____ at the circus. (clowns//skaters)
7. There was a lot of salt _____. (on the vegetables//on the meat)
8. There was a light on _____. (in the bedroom//in the living room)
9. There are seats _____. (for the reporters//for the photographers)
10. There'll be an election _____. (next year//this year)
11. There's a soup bowl _____. (on the shelf//on the counter)
12. There's room for two people _____. (on this seat//on that seat)

C. Form affirmative and negative sentences about the picture. Use **there** and a form of **be**.

Ex. (blood)
There's blood on the sofa.

1. (a broken vase)
2. (a knife)
3. (flowers)
4. (photographers)
5. (a fight)

86 There Sentences: Questions and Short Answers

Is	there a picture on the wall?	Yes,	there is.
Are	there five pictures on the wall?	No,	there aren't.
Will	there be a clock on the wall?	Yes,	there will.

A. Form sentences like the model. Substitute the subject, the tense of **be**, or the complement. Use the correct singular or plural form of **be**. Do 1–12 in order.

<u>Is there a bank on Main Street?</u>

Ex. bus stops
Are there bus stops on Main Street?

1. in Rockville
2. a sports field
3. was
4. fireworks
5. will be
6. a parade
7. downtown
8. is going to be
9. in the park
10. speeches
11. were
12. dancing

B. Answer the questions with short answers.

Ex. Will there be an election next year?
No, **there won't.**

1. Is there a tiger in the zoo? Yes, _____.
2. Are there any penguins in the zoo? No, _____.
3. Was there any time for review? Yes, _____.
4. Were there many mistakes on this test paper? No, _____.
5. Will there be a lot of snow on the ground? Yes, _____.
6. Is there going to be a picture of the winner? No, _____.
7. Are there forty seats on this bus? Yes, _____.
8. Will there be many accidents over the weekend? No, _____.
9. Is there ice cream for dessert? Yes, _____.
10. Was there a storm last night? No, _____.
11. Are there going to be any horses in the parade? Yes, _____.

C. Study the picture. Student 1: ask a yes/no question about the subjects in parentheses. Student 2: give a short **yes** or **no** answer.

Ex. (a circus)
Is there a circus in Rockville? No, there isn't.
(or) **Is there going to be a circus in Rockville. Yes, there is.**

1. (a circus parade)
2. (elephants)
3. (fireworks)
4. (clowns)
5. (leopards)

87 Question Word Questions: who and what as Subject

What is/**what's** in that closet?
Who is/**who's** talking?
Who closed the door?

A. Form sentences like the model. Substitute **who** or **what** as the subject or the verb phrase. Do 1-12 in order.

   Who is playing on the floor?

Ex. will work
Who'll work on the floor?

1. is rolling
2. What
3. fell
4. was lying
5. Who
6. writes
7. didn't sit
8. wasn't sitting
9. wants to sleep
10. is going to sit
11. made these marks
12. What

B. Student 1: read the sentence. Ask a **who** or **what** question like the example. Student 2: give a short answer.

Ex. Joyce brought the salad. (the cake//Helen)
Who brought the cake? Helen did.

1. My mother told part of the story. (the whole story//My father)
2. A librarian works in a library. (in a restaurant//A waiter)
3. Dorothy was in the living room. (on the porch//Betty)
4. Water was ruining the car doors. (the plastic roof//The sun)
5. Elephants are big and gray. (little and gray//Mice)
6. Leopards have spots. (stripes//Tigers)
7. The carpenter will fix the roof. (the lights//The electrician)
8. Oliver owns that blue car. (that green car//Earl)
9. A saw cuts wood. (paper//A scissors)
10. *Gone With the Wind* is playing at the Bijou Theater. (at the Palace//*War and Peace*)
11. Lawyers go to law school. (medical school//Doctors)

C. Student 1: ask **who** and **what** questions about each picture. Student 2: answer the questions.

1. **What's falling? Garbage is.**
   Who's running? Some kids are.

88 Question Word Questions: who and what as Object

What did she eat for supper?
What are you looking at?
Who/Whom is he taking to the dance?

A. Form questions like the example. Put the words in the correct order.

Ex. at the sale/buy/did/he/what
What did he buy at the sale?

1. did/in the closet/put/what/you
2. did/meet/on the bus/she/who
3. does/in her free time/make/she/what
4. do/in that room/keep/they/what
5. are/sending/they/to the conference/who
6. he/in the newspaper/is/reading/what
7. for the picnic/is/making/she/what
8. about/ask/it/who/will/you
9. going to/he/help/is/on Saturday/who
10. about her trip/Bonnie/telling/was/who
11. about/fighting/they/were/what
12. are/for/looking/who/you
13. did/Pat/play chess/who/with
14. change/going to/into/is/she/what

B. Student 1: read each sentence. Ask a **who** (**whom**) or **what** question like the example. Student 2: give a short answer.

Ex. Nancy made the curtains. (Paula//the doll)
What did Paula make? She made the doll.

1. Barbara baked a cake. (Helen//bread)
2. I like chocolate ice cream. (you//strawberry ice cream)
3. Mr. Hien is studying English. (Mr. Anh//French)
4. Bill's going to invite Betty. (Stan//Stella)
5. Miss Benson lost a sock. (Phil//his toothbrush)
6. I'm ordering meat. (you//fish)
7. Joe looks like his mother. (Mary//her father)
8. I'll paint the ceiling. (Hank//the walls)
9. Amanda wants to sit on the chair. (Nicole//the rug)
10. Amanda thanked Mr. Benson. (Nicole//Mrs. Benson)
11. We're waiting for the number 3 bus. (those people//the number 5 bus)

C. Form questions like the examples about the picture. Use **who** (**whom**) or **what** and one of the verbs.

Ex. A. What's in the top drawer?
Ex. B. Who's the girl talking to?

eat   keep   take out   wear
go   receive talk   be

89 Question Word Questions: which

Which knife/one { is yours? / will cut this rope? / are you using? / did he step on? }

A. Form sentences like the model. Substitute the subject or the verb phrase. Do 1-12 in order.

Which camera <u>did</u> <u>Ben</u> <u>lose</u>?

Ex. is using
Which camera is <u>Ben</u> using?

1. they
2. were using
3. she
4. will get
5. you
6. do like
7. are keeping
8. Mr. Kidd
9. did break
10. is going to take
11. the Turners
12. do want to sell

B. Student 1: read the sentence. Student 2: ask a question like the example. Use **which one** or **which ones**. Student 1: then answer the question.

Ex. Tony took a dessert. (the apple pie)
Which one did he take? The apple pie.

1. The maid locked two doors? (Rooms 506 and 508)
2. Sue's painting a bedroom. (Judy's bedroom)
3. I broke my arm. (my left arm)
4. He read some chapters. (Chapters 5 through 7)
5. We'll learn some of the poems. (the first, third, and sixth)
6. She was climbing through a window. (the kitchen window)
7. He wants to join a team. (the soccer team)
8. They're going to change some rugs. (the living room and hall rugs)
9. We list some names. (the winners)
10. I'll take a magazine. (*Time*)
11. He visits many cities. (Newark, Hoboken, and Paterson)

C. Student 1: ask questions about the bus directory. Use **which**. Student 2: answer the questions.

Ex. Which gate does Bus 8 stop at? Gate D.

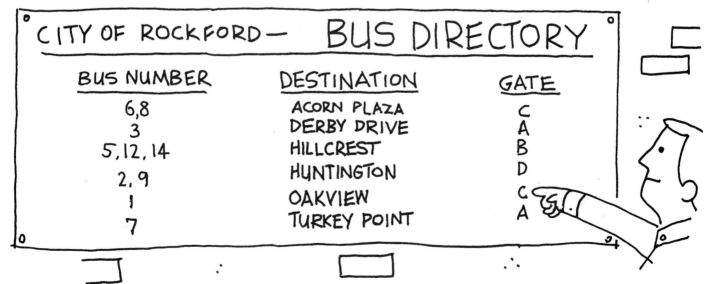

BUS NUMBER	DESTINATION	GATE
6, 8	ACORN PLAZA	C
3	DERBY DRIVE	A
5, 12, 14	HILLCREST	B
2, 9	HUNTINGTON	D
1	OAKVIEW	C
7	TURKEY POINT	A

90 Question Word Questions: whose

Whose (knife) { will cut this rope?
are you using?
did he step on? }

A. Match 1-8 with a-h to form questions.

1. Whose brother
2. Whose grade
3. Whose handbag
4. Whose house
5. Whose records
6. Whose room
7. Whose shoes
8. Whose voice

a. are you going to paint blue?
b. burned to the ground?
c. did they open?
d. is Jason?
e. is over 90?
f. sounds good?
g. are size 7?
h. will they play at the party?

B. Read the statement. Then form a question like the example. Use **whose** as a pronoun.

Ex. I didn't ride John's bicycle.
Whose did you ride?

1. I didn't use Jane's typewriter.
2. We don't swim in our pool.
3. Carey doesn't want Jim's kite.
4. Sue isn't going to take Sal's picture.
5. Pete wasn't wearing Mark's cap.
6. Paul didn't fill your glass.
7. Heather didn't drink from Pam's cup.
8. Lynn won't stay at Dawn's house.
9. Kurt isn't carrying Gail's books.
10. I'm not fixing Norman's watch.

C. Study the picture. Two college men live in this room. Fred's an engineering student; Roger's studying history. Student 1: ask questions about subjects 1-10. Student 2: answer each question.

Ex. (belt)
Whose belt is that? It's Fred's.

1. (history book)
2. (girlfriend)
3. (glasses)
4. (calculator)
5. (water glass)
6. (camera)
7. (radio)
8. (coat)
9. (letters)
10. (cookies)

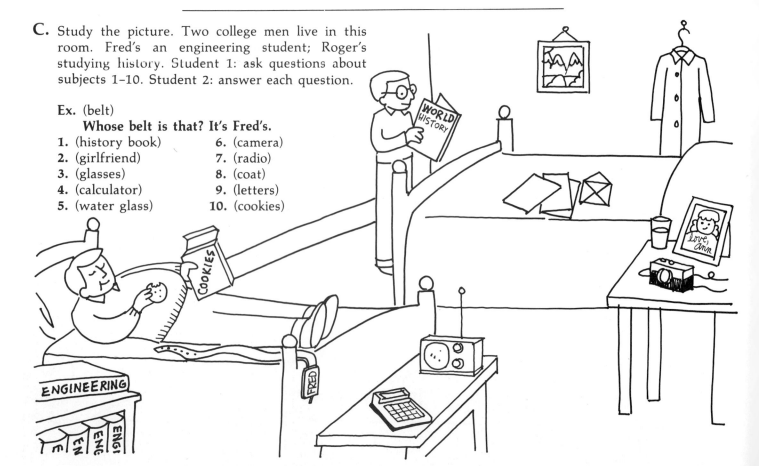

91 Question Word Questions: *where*

Where { is my pen?
        were you sitting?
        did he eat his lunch?

A. Student 1: Form sentences like the model. Substitute the verb phrase or subject. Student 2: ask a **where** question. Student 1: then answer **In the kitchen**. Do 1-12 in order.

He is cooking eggs. Where's he cooking them?
In the kitchen.

Ex. cooks
He cooks eggs. Where does he cook them? In the kitchen.

1. will cook
2. cooked
3. is going to cook
4. they
5. cook
6. were cooking
7. are cooking
8. I
9. was cooking
10. cooked
11. want to cook
12. she

1. Miss Alexander was in Hong Kong. (Miss Hinders//Bangkok)
2. Lions live in Africa. (tigers//Southeast Asia)
3. Ron parked in the parking lot. (Don//on the street)
4. The Statue of Liberty is in New York. (the White House//Washington)
5. Towels are on the fifth floor. (toys//the seventh floor)
6. The car show will be in Dallas. (the boat show//Houston)
7. Dave was living on Walnut Street. (John//Elm Street)
8. Our children were playing in our yard. (their kids//the neighbor's)
9. I'm wearing the pin on my left side. (she//her right side)
10. Mr. Young is going to teach in Newark. (Mr. Lachowicz//Detroit)
11. The Japanese tourists are going to New York City. (the German tourists//the southwestern states)

B. Student 1: read the sentence. Then ask a **where** question like the example. Student 2: answer the question.

Ex. Jason eats lunch at the cafeteria. (Helen//at the sandwich shop)
Where does Helen eat lunch?
At the sandwich shop.

C. Student 1: ask **where** questions like the example about the picture. Use the present tense. Student 2: answer the questions.

Ex. (read the newspaper)
Where does Mr. Crooks read the newspaper?
In the living room.

1. (play cards)
2. (eat dinner)
3. (do homework)
4. (take baths)
5. (watch TV)
6. (sleep)
7. (keep the bird)
8. (write letters)
9. (have the phone)

92 Question Word Questions: when

When { was the game?
does she get up?
did they go to the pool? }

A. Student 1: form sentences like the model. Substitute the verb phrase or subject in the statement. Student 2: ask a **when** question. Student 1: then answer **In the morning**. Do 1-12 in order.

She reads the newspaper. When **does she read** it? In the morning.

Ex. read (past tense)
She read the newspaper. When did she read it? In the morning.

1. is going to read
2. will read
3. They
4. read (present)
5. are going to read
6. I
7. read (present)
8. will read
9. read (past)
10. We
11. will read
12. are going to read

B. Student 1: read the sentence. Student 2: ask a **when** question like the example about it. Student 1: then answer the question.

Ex. Dawn will return to class. (next week)
When will she return? Next week.

1. The sky will clear up. (this afternoon)
2. He was at the dentist's. (on Tuesday)
3. Miss Tyler cut her hair. (yesterday)
4. I was feeling bad. (in the morning)
5. Some people were leaving. (at 9:00)
6. We get snow. (in January and February)
7. Fresh fruit will be in the stores. (tomorrow morning)
8. The neighbors got angry. (last night)
9. She changes the sheets. (on Mondays)
10. The price is going to go up. (in March)
11. The driver wants to take a rest. (now)

C. Study the picture. Mr. Finsterbush is in his office. It is now 11:30 a.m. Student 1: ask **when** questions like the example about Mr. Finsterbush's appointments. Student 2: answer. Use a time expression.

Ex. (be at the sales meeting)
When was Mr. Finsterbush at the sales meeting? At 9:30.

1. (call his wife)
2. (interview Miss Adams)
3. (go for lunch)
4. (call Atlanta)
5. (call Sal)

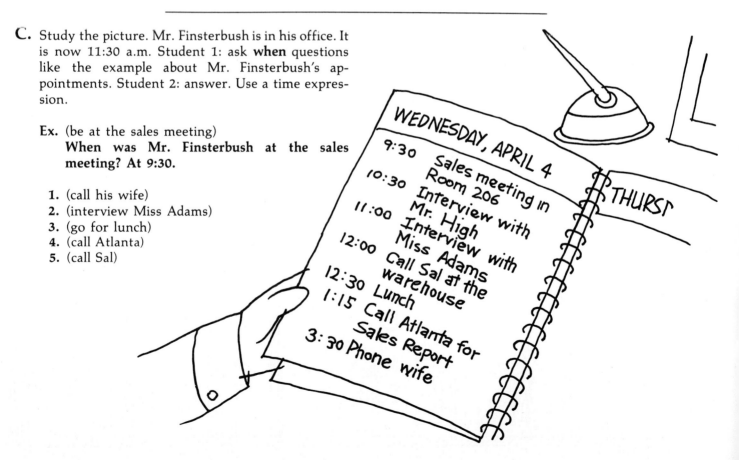

93 Question Word Questions: how many and how much

How many (books) { are falling? / is she picking up? }

How much (milk) { spilled? / did he spill? }

A. Form sentences like the model. Substitute the subject or the verb. Use **how many** or **how much**. Do 1–12 in order.

How many <u>shirts</u> <u>were</u> in the box?

Ex. sand
How much sand was in the box?

1. toys
2. rice
3. mice
4. money
5. coins
6. will go
7. bottles
8. wood
9. did you put
10. socks
11. food
12. is

B. Student 1: read the sentence. Student 2: ask a question using **how many** or **how much**. Student 1: then answer the question like the example.

Ex. Tony drank some coffee. (two cups)
How much did he drink? Two cups.

1. She's learning some new words every day. (a dozen)
2. I see some children. (nine or ten)
3. He bought some paper. (about 200 sheets)
4. They'll need some chairs. (about twenty)
5. I'm going to buy some candles. (about fifty)
6. Some milk went bad. (about half of it)
7. She didn't find some addresses. (four)
8. Some people drank tea. (six)
9. Some juice wasn't good. (two or three glasses)
10. Some coats are lying on the sofa. (about ten)
11. Some trees were down after the storm. (five or six)

C. Student 1: ask **how many** and **how much** questions about the picture. Student 2: answer each question with a quantity expression.

Ex. **How many police cars are at the accident? Two.**

94 Question Word Questions: Summary

Who	Which	Where	How many
What	Whose	When	How much

A. Read the paragraph. Then fill in the blanks with question words. Give short answers.

Bob Safely and Harold Koop went camping in the Green Mountains last July 5. They carried 35 pounds of food, extra clothes, and Harold's tent on their backs. The scenery and weather were beautiful at first. Then it became rainy. On the eleventh they were climbing near Steep Rock. Harold fell. He broke his left leg. Bob went for help. They got out the next day.

1. <u>Who</u> went camping?
   Bob Safely and Harold Koop did.
2. _____ had an accident?
3. _____ did they sleep in?
4. _____ tent did they use?
5. _____ food did they take?
6. _____ did Harold fall?
7. _____ leg did he break?
8. _____ did they get back?
9. _____ were they away?

B. Student 1: ask question word questions like the example about the picture. Student 2: answer each question.

**Ex. What's the old woman holding?
She's holding an umbrella.**

C. Student 1: read the sentence. Student 2: ask a question word question about the sentence. Student 1: answer the question.

**Ex. I need some 25-cent stamps.
How many do you need? About ten.**

1. He brought a school book along.
2. We'll go in one car.
3. Bill drank some chocolate milk.
4. I lost my glove.
5. I gave away your red necktie.
6. We're going to have a test.
7. It rained one day on our vacation.
8. I looked at new cars today.

95 Tag Questions with the Verb be

He is/'s a bus driver, **isn't he?**
She isn't a pilot, **is she?**

A. Form sentences like the model. Substitute the subject or the form of **be**. Use the correct form of the tag question. Do 1–12 in order.

<u>She is cold</u>, **isn't she?**

Ex. isn't
She isn't cold, is she?

1. They
2. are
3. were
4. It
5. wasn't
6. isn't
7. is
8. will be
9. He
10. won't be
11. You
12. I

B. Student 1: add a tag question to each statement. Student 2: give a short **yes** or **no** answer. The answer will agree with the statement.

Ex. A penguin is a bird, **isn't it? Yes, it is.**

1. The airplane isn't ready.
2. This car is a taxi.
3. You aren't a Texan.
4. The apples are ripe.
5. Eric will be a barber soon.
6. Your pencil wasn't very sharp.
7. The game was in New York City.
8. All the windows were square.
9. The fish weren't in a big bowl.
10. The owner won't be late.
11. The lions are in their cage.
12. My hat is on right.
13. Your clothes aren't from Paris.
14. I'm almost done.

C. Study the picture. Student 1: ask tag questions like the example about subjects 1–4. Student 2: give a short **yes** or **no** answer.

Ex. (Gretchen)
Gretchen's a teenager, isn't she? Yes, she is.

1. (her clothes)
2. (her father)
3. (the record)
4. (her hair)

96 Tag Questions with Continuous Tenses

They were working yesterday, **weren't they?**
They aren't working now, **are they?**

A. Form sentences like the model. Substitute the subject or the verb phrase. Use the correct form of the tag question. Do 1-12 in order.

<u>Mr. Jenks was riding</u> in the car, **wasn't he?**

Ex. isn't riding
Mr. Jenks isn't riding in the car, is he?

1. The dogs
2. aren't sleeping
3. Clara
4. is reading
5. Clara and you
6. aren't fighting
7. were singing
8. The driver
9. isn't singing
10. is laughing
11. The children
12. are telling jokes

B. Read this paragraph. Student 1: ask tag questions about it. Use verbs 1-12 in a continuous tense. Student 2: give a short **yes** or **no** answer.

Jeff was tired and hungry after his soccer game. He sat on the living room sofa and waited. His mother was getting supper ready. She was making noise. Soon he was asleep. Then he saw great flying animals. They appeared over a hill and came straight toward him. Their voices sounded like airplane engines, and they called his name. They all landed on the ground and sounded like a storm at the ocean. One reached out and caught his neck. He didn't move. He woke up and his mother was there. "Aren't you hungry, Jeff? Supper's getting cold," she said.

Ex. (wait)
**Jeff was waiting for supper, wasn't he?
Yes, he was.**

1. (sit)
2. (feel)
3. (read)
4. (sleep)
5. (cook)
6. (wash)
7. (come)
8. (talk)
9. (watch)
10. (lift)
11. (hold)
12. (eat)

C. Study the picture. Student 1: form a negative statement about subjects 1-4. Add a tag question. Student 2: give a short **no** answer. Then give the correct information from a-d.

1. The clowns
2. The dog
3. The lady
4. The monkeys

a. climb on the car.
b. jump over fire.
c. ride bicycles.
d. walk on a rope.

1. **The clowns aren't riding bicycles, are they?
No, they aren't. They're climbing on the car.**

97 Tag Questions with the Auxiliary do

You (do) like Joyce now, **don't you?**
You didn't like her before, **did you?**

A. Form sentences like the model. Substitute the subject and verb phrase. Use the correct form of the tag question. Do 1–12 in order.

He <u>drank</u> <u>milk</u>, **didn't he?**

Ex. drinks
He drinks milk, doesn't he?

1. You
2. didn't drink
3. don't like
4. She
5. bought
6. didn't have
7. They
8. use
9. don't need
10. wanted
11. The baby
12. needs

B. Student 1: add a tag question to the statement. Student 2: give a short **yes** or **no** answer. The answer will agree with the statement.

Ex. Miss Clark has a camera, **doesn't she?**
Yes, she does.

1. Your brother has a watch.
2. Many people don't like Bill.
3. She didn't wash this window.
4. Buses stop here.
5. Ralph always takes the bus.
6. A cup and saucer broke.
7. He found ice in the bowl.
8. The curtains didn't get yellow.
9. This restaurant doesn't serve beer.
10. You parked in the wrong place.
11. The boss wants to change the name.
12. You didn't change the calendar.
13. Mrs. Taylor worked hard all day.
14. The flag has fifty stars on it.

C. Study the picture. Student 1: ask tag questions like the example. Use verbs 1–4. Student 2: give a short answer.

Ex. (like)
Danny doesn't like airplanes, does he?
Yes, he does.

1. (draw)
2. (win)
3. (play)
4. (listen to)

98 Tag Questions with there Sentences

There's some butter on the table, **isn't there?**
There aren't any apples on the table, **are there?**

A. Student 1: ask tag questions like the example about ingredients 1-9 in the recipe. Use **there** in subject position. Student 2: give a short **yes** or **no** answer.

Ex. salt
There's salt in the cake, isn't there?
Yes, there is.

1. eggs
2. nuts
3. butter
4. raisins
5. chocolate
6. salt
7. milk
8. berries
9. brown sugar

LAYERCAKE
2 Eggs
1 cup sugar
½ cup butter
2 squares chocolate
½ cup milk
½ tsp. baking soda
2 cups flour
vanilla

Blend ingredients.
Bake 25 min. at 350°.

B. Fill in the blanks with the tag question or **there** and a form of **be**.

1. There's a black bird on the roof, <u>isn't there</u>?
2. There aren't any clouds in the sky, _____?
3. There'll be snow on the ground soon, _____?
4. There are towels in the bathroom, _____?
5. There are no yellow flowers in the garden, _____?
6. There was some sand in the box, _____?
7. There weren't any bad storms last winter, _____?
8. _____ a lock on the door, was there?
9. There were some big closets in that house, _____?
10. _____ a map on the back seat, isn't there?
11. _____ a small animal in his hand, wasn't there?
12. There will be a lot of people at the meeting, _____?

C. Student 1: ask tag questions like the example about subjects in the pictures. Use **there** in sentences with various tenses. Student 2: give short **yes** or **no** answers.

Ex. (drugstore)
There was a drugstore on the corner of Main Street in 1946, wasn't there? Yes, there was. (or)
There isn't a drugstore on First Avenue now, is there? No, there isn't.

1. (tall buildings)
2. (post office)
3. (people)
4. (bank)

99 Tag Questions: Summary

> He is . . . , **isn't he**?
> They will . . . , **won't they**?
> She wasn't . . . , **was she**?
> You didn't . . . , **did you**?

A. Form tag questions like the example.

Ex. Ralph likes kites.
Ralph likes kites, doesn't he?

1. He doesn't have any kites from Singapore.
2. Professor Brown caught a cold.
3. He was running in the rain.
4. The Garcias take a long trip every year.
5. Mrs. Garcia didn't go to Morocco last year.
6. The car is a Volkswagen.
7. Those cars are very old.
8. You didn't burn the leaves.
9. The leaves are still on the ground.
10. The meeting wasn't at 11:00 o'clock.
11. The speaker won't be late again.
12. There aren't any tomatoes in this salad.
13. You didn't put any tomatoes in this salad.
14. Your brothers weren't in the house.
15. They left the door open.
16. There's a reason for their mistake.
17. They weren't listening to the directions.
18. The game lasted four hours.
19. We'll go home right away.
20. Jason is taking a long time.
21. Ginny is not going to wait for him.

B. Study the picture. Student 1: ask tag questions like the example. Use verbs 1-6 in various tenses. Student 2: answer the questions.

Ex. (There's)
There's a sign on the cash register, isn't there?
Yes, there is.

1. (buy)
2. (get)
3. (like)
4. (read)
5. (give)
6. (there are)

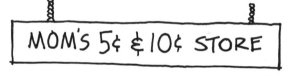

100 Negative Questions with the Verb be

Isn't Perry a pilot?
Weren't the kids crying?

A. Form sentences like the model. Student 1: substitute the subject and the complement in the question. Use **isn't** or **aren't**. Student 2: give a short **yes** or **no** answer. Do 1–12 in order.

Isn't Mr. O'Brien Irish? **Yes, he is.**

Ex. the Hochs//No
Aren't the Hochs Irish? No, they aren't.

1. from Ireland//No
2. Marie//No
3. tall//Yes
4. Charles//No
5. the carpenter//Yes
6. on the roof//No
7. the nails//No
8. in your pocket//Yes
9. the key//Yes
10. new//No
11. those shoes//Yes
12. your good shoes//Yes

B. Study the pictures. Student 1: ask a negative question like the example. Use **wasn't** or **weren't**. Student 2: answer **no** and give the correct information.

Ex. the painter's name/Frank
**Wasn't the painter's name Frank?
No, it was Henry.**

1. that meat/$1.29
2. your socks/in the bottom drawer
3. that woman/Italian
4. Mrs. Frazer/in Room 423
5. the cups/empty
6. the vegetables/peas
7. the berries/sweet

C. Respond to the statements like the example. Use negative questions.

Ex. The carpenters are working. (rest)
Oh, aren't they resting?

1. The temperature's going down today. (rise)
2. Tina's talking on the phone. (study)
3. Pete's painting the hall. (paint the kitchen)
4. The birds are going north. (stay here)
5. Mr. and Mrs. Jones are singing tonight. (sing tomorrow night)
6. George was flying a kite. (swim)
7. My aunt was teaching French. (teach English)
8. The potatoes were boiling in the pot. (bake in the oven)
9. They were putting up a stop sign. (put up a traffic light)

101 Negative Questions with the Auxiliary do

Doesn't Joe feel well?
Don't you have the key?

A. Form sentences like the model. Substitute the subject or the verb and complement. Use **don't** or **doesn't**. Do 1-12 in order.

Don't <u>they</u> <u>fix radios</u>?

Ex. Mr. Clark
Doesn't Mr. Clark fix radios?

1. speak German
2. those people
3. come from Germany
4. Klaus
5. want a sandwich
6. know John's address
7. live on Maple Street
8. the Jacksons
9. have two cars
10. Marcia
11. play the guitar
12. your brothers

B. Student 1: ask a negative question about each picture. Use **doesn't**, **don't**, or **didn't**. Student 2: answer **no** and give the correct information.

Ex. Barbara and Jane/shop/at Woodward's
**Didn't Barbara and Jane shop at Woodward's?
No, they shopped at Sandler's.**

1. Henry/paint/pictures
2. Tigers/live/in Africa
3. Mrs. Thorpe/work/in a factory
4. Clara/buy/her clothes
5. the children/want/candy
6. the bank/open/at 9 o'clock
7. the Marinos/go/to the beach

C. Respond to the statements with negative questions. Study the example.

Ex. I don't know the time. (have a watch)
Oh, don't you have a watch?

1. I won't have any pie. (like pie)
2. This pen is no good. (have ink in it)
3. The stores aren't open yet. (open at 9 o'clock)
4. The workers left. (finish their job)
5. The Parkers moved to Glen Rock. (get jobs there)
6. Mrs. Baker stayed in all day. (walk in the park in the afternoon)
7. Jane got wet feet. (wear boots)
8. Darrell is going to study tonight. (want to go to the movies)
9. I don't want more pie. (taste good)

102 Adverbials: Place

at 1600 Pennsylvania Avenue
on Pennsylvania Avenue
in Washington, D.C.

A. Form sentences like the model. Substitute the place expression. Use **at, on,** or **in**.

He lived **in** Detroit.

Ex. Joliet Street
He lived on Joliet Street.

1. 361 Joliet Street
2. Michigan (a state)
3. the United States
4. Holland Avenue
5. Rockport (a town)
6. the River Road Apartment Building
7. River Road
8. that house
9. a crossroad
10. a big street
11. a small city
12. my neighborhood

B. Study the pictures. Fill in the blanks with prepositions from the list or no preposition. Mark "X" for no preposition.

| at | in | off | on | out of |
| away from | into | off of | onto | to |

1. A boy was sitting __on__ a rock. He saw a big dog and ran _____ it. He ran _____ home. He got _____ the front door and ran _____ the house.
2. I took the boiling pot _____ the stove and poured the soup _____ it _____ a clean bowl. The soup was hot. I left it _____ the bowl for a while.
3. A lady heard a loud noise _____ the road _____ back of her car. She stopped _____ the next corner and got _____ the car. A hub cap was lying _____ the grass. She picked it up and put it _____ the back seat.
4. Bev had an accident _____ the office. She spilled coffee _____ her dress. She got a cloth _____ the desk drawer. Then she went _____ the ladies' room and put water _____ the cloth. That didn't work. The coffee stain was still _____ the dress.

103 Adverbials: Time

yesterday/last week	before noon/Friday/June	at noon
today/this week	after noon/Friday/June	on Friday
tomorrow/next week		in June

A. Form sentences like the model. Substitute the time expression. Use the past tense, present continuous, or **will** future.

They're **moving** <u>this week</u>.

Ex. next month
They'll move next month.

1. today
2. yesterday
3. tomorrow
4. next year
5. this year
6. last year
7. tonight
8. yesterday morning
9. this month
10. tomorrow morning
11. last week
12. tomorrow night

B. Answer each question with a short **no** answer. Then form an affirmative statement with **at, on,** or **in**.

Ex. Will he come before Sunday?
No, he won't. He'll come on Sunday.

1. Will he come after 3:00 o'clock?
2. Will they start before March?
3. Will they start after 1988?
4. Did she call before his birthday?
5. Did she call after midnight?
6. Did you buy it before 1975?
7. Did you buy it after January?
8. Does the train leave before 10:00?
9. Does he need it before the first of the month?
10. Do we need it before Tuesday?
11. Do we need it after the first of the month?

C. Student 1: Do not look at the pictures. Complete the question. Use a time expression. Student 2: answer the question. Give the correct information from the pictures.

1. Will the alarm clock ring (**time**)?
   Will the alarm clock ring at 7:00?
   No, it'll ring at 5:30.
   Are you getting up _____(time)_____ ?
2. Will they be away _____(month)_____ ?
   Are they going to leave _____(day)_____ ?
3. Was Edison born _____(year)_____ ?
   Did Lindbergh die _____(month and year)_____ ?

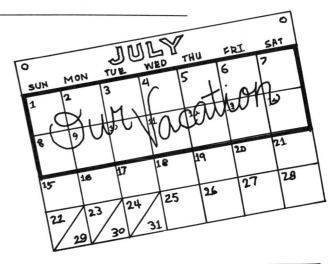

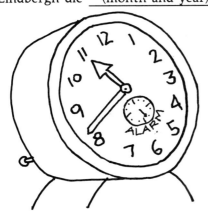

Thomas Edison   1847–1931

Charles Lindbergh   1902–1974

104 Adverbials: Order of Place and Time

He spent $50 **at the restaurant   last night.**

A. Form sentences like the model. Substitute the place or time expressions. Do 1–12 in order.

   She enjoyed herself <u>at the museum</u> <u>yesterday</u>.

Ex. downtown
   She enjoyed herself downtown yesterday.

1. the other day
2. in Little Rock
3. last week
4. at the farm
5. this summer
6. on the beach
7. all afternoon
8. in the park
9. at lunchtime
10. in the playground
11. for an hour
12. away from the office

B. Complete the sentences like the example. Put the place and time expressions in the correct order.

   Ex. She doesn't have lettuce ____. (in her garden/right now) **She doesn't have lettuce in her garden right now.**

1. He landed ____. (at 1:30/in Cairo)
2. That truck will stay ____. (in the garage/tomorrow)
3. He spent the month of March ____. (in the hospital/last year)
4. John sleeps ____. (downstairs/in the winter)
5. I left my camera ____. (April 13/in the post office)
6. We're going to get ____. (a few days from now/to Yellowstone)
7. Mr. Underwood lived ____. (for three years/in Louisiana)
8. No milk was ____. (after breakfast/in the refrigerator)
9. He took some change ____. (immediately/out of his pocket)
10. There weren't many tourists ____. (at the beach/this summer)
11. She planted some flowers ____. (before dark/by the front door)
12. They had a play ____. (Friday night/in school)
13. They're putting up notices about the election ____. (all over town/this evening)
14. The neighbors had a party ____. (a few days ago/in their back yard)

C. Form sentences about each picture. Use a place and a time expression. Use the present tense with picture 1, **will** future with picture 2, and past tense with picture 3.

1. **A bus leaves for Little Rock at 3:55.**
   (or) **A bus arrives from Little Rock at 2:55.**

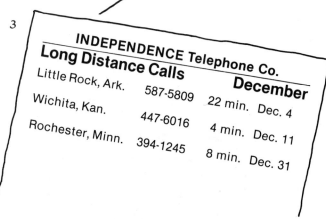

105 Adverbials: Frequency

always	usually	often
never	seldom	sometimes

A. Form sentences like the model. Substitute the frequency adverb (in medial position) or the verb phrase. Do 1–12 in order.

   She <u>doesn't</u> <u>often</u> <u>look</u> at Dan's picture.

   Ex. looks
   She often looks at Dan's picture.

   1. seldom
   2. always
   3. didn't look
   4. usually
   5. was looking
   6. sometimes
   7. never
   8. looked
   9. seldom
   10. often
   11. wasn't looking
   12. always

B. Add the frequency adverbial in parentheses to these sentences.

   Ex. They're wrong about the weather. (seldom)
   They're seldom wrong about the weather.

   1. Our bank account is low. (always)
   2. The children were hungry at five o'clock. (usually)
   3. He was a dishwasher at that restaurant. (never)
   4. The dog is waiting by the door. (often)
   5. Miss Truce is going to miss her old friends in Altad. (sometimes)
   6. I'm going to stay out after midnight. (never)
   7. They ask for your license number. (always) (always)
   8. Mr. Traub parks his car on the street. (sometimes)
   9. Fanny leaves the office at 5:30. (always)
   10. We locked our doors at night. (seldom)
   11. Planes flew over the city. (often)
   12. They'll take a late payment. (sometimes)
   13. People change trains at Redrock. (usually)

C. Student 1: ask yes/no questions like the example about the student's English grades. Use the word **ever**. Student 2: answer the questions.

   Ex. Did Francisco get A on a test last year? No, he never did. Did Maria get A on a test last year? Yes, but she seldom did.

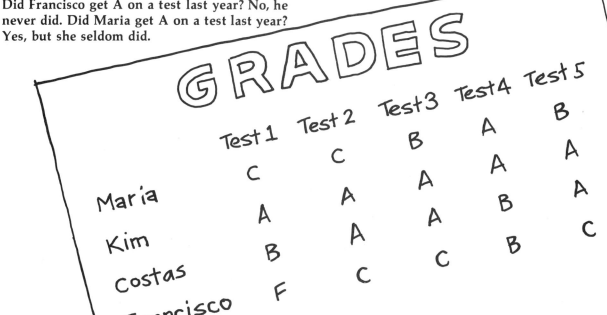

106 Conjunctions: and

Juan is Spanish, **and** Jean is French.
John went to Spain, **and** (he) learned Spanish.

A. Fill in the blanks with **and** and words from the first part of the sentence.

1. Sean is Irish, __and__ Ivan __is__ Russian.
2. Haruo has an American wife, _____ Harry _____ a Japanese wife.
3. The Giants are playing in Pittsburgh, _____ the Yankees _____ here.
4. Ted reads the sports page, _____ Dennis _____ the business page.
5. I ate the apple, _____ Mary _____ the orange.
6. We're going to the circus on Tuesday, _____ they _____ a soccer game.
7. I took off my shoes, _____ Kay _____ my socks.
8. Mr. Walker ordered the pens, _____ Miss Butterfield _____ the paper.
9. Betty sells houses, _____ her husband _____ furniture.
10. Mrs. MacDonald comes from Salinas, _____ Mr. Romig _____ Anaheim.
11. Meat was cooking in the oven, _____ corn _____ on the stove.
12. Mr. Munger left his watch home, _____ Don _____ his umbrella _____ .

B. Form sentences like the example. Use **and**.

Ex. Laura/is putting on shorts/is taking off her skirt
Laura is taking off her skirt and putting on shorts.

1. The mailman/brought us two letters and a magazine/came
2. Esther/was eating cake/was sitting at the table
3. Buses/pick up passengers/stop on that corner
4. Mr. Dunbar/brought balloons/gave balloons (them) to the kids
5. Miss Hoff/got a sunburn/was on the beach all day
6. Mrs. Boyd/will paint the room/will wash out the brushes
7. Miss Cummings/cleaned the blackboard for the teacher/sat down
8. Donald/is a doctor/works at football games
9. They/locked the car/parked the car (it) for the night
10. Ruth/bought apples/made an apple pie
11. We have to/catch the dog/give the dog (it) a bath

C. Form sentences about the picture. Use full clauses and the word **and**.

Ex. **The Troutens went fishing, and the Powells went to the beach.**

107 Conjunctions: but

Juan is Spanish, **but** Jean is French.
John is lying down, **but** he isn't sleeping.

A. Complete the sentences. Form a **but** clause with the words in parentheses.

Ex. Math is easy for me, _____. (are/but/for me/hard/languages)
Math is easy for me, but languages are hard for me.

1. Lucy used scissors, _____. (a knife/but/Clara/used)
2. Mark's afraid of high places, _____. (afraid of/Allen/but/dark places/is)
3. Paul wants to play soccer, _____. (basketball/Ben//but/to play/wants)
4. The envelopes have letters in them, _____. (but/don't/have/pictures/they)
5. Frank ate all his food, _____. (doesn't/well/feel/he/but)
6. Santa Barbara is by the ocean, _____. (Bakersfield/but/in the valley/is)

B. Complete the sentences after **but**. Choose a clause from the parentheses.

Ex. Juan is Spanish, but _____. (he's from Valencia/he isn't from Madrid)
Juan is Spanish, but **he isn't from Madrid.**

1. The baby can stand, but _____. (she can sit up/she can't walk)
2. The car is dirty, but _____. (I'm not going to wash it/it needs a washing)
3. Mark likes California girls, but _____. (Mark doesn't like them/Mark doesn't like California)
4. She walks to the post office, but _____. (she drives to the library/she walks to the library)
5. He emptied the wastebasket, but _____. (I took some papers out of it/he didn't put it back under the desk)
6. Henry spilled the coffee, but _____. (Florence cleaned it up/he didn't drink it first)
7. Archie wants to skate, but _____. (he wants to go outside/Frank has his skates)
8. Mr. Grosh worked hard, but _____. (he didn't earn much money/he worked at a furniture company)

C. Complete the sentences about each picture. Use **but** and a clause.

1. Mr. Gunnett was hungry,
   but the refrigerator was empty.
2. Miss Holton had some 15-cent stamps, _____.
3. Nancy Dettling is a good student, _____.
4. They changed the street light, _____.
5. I didn't go to the parade, _____.
6. Dombrowski played in the game, _____.

108 Conjunctions: but in Short Clauses

Juan is Spanish, **but** Jean isn't.
Juan didn't study here, **but** Jean did.

A. Complete the sentences like the example. Use **but** and a clause with the words in parentheses.

Ex. Mildred lives in Rock City, **but Claire doesn't.** (Claire)

1. Harold isn't fishing today, _____. (Tom)
2. My umbrella is in the closet, _____. (my boots)
3. The book didn't have a happy ending, _____. (the movie)
4. Mrs. Kozy's eyeglasses broke, _____. (her watch)
5. The parents were tired, _____. (the children)
6. Miss Zimmerman is almost ready, _____. (I)
7. Marie wasn't playing well, _____. (Barbara)
8. White shirts show the dirt easily, _____. (dark shirts)
9. Crows can fly, _____. (penguins)
10. The neighbor's dog barked all night, _____. (ours)
11. The five o'clock bus will be late, _____. (the 5:30 bus)
12. This door won't open, _____. (that one)
13. The bookstore doesn't have writing paper, _____. (the drugstore)

B. Answer each question like the example. Use a full sentence with **but not** and a short clause.

Ex. Does Mildred live in Rock City? (Claire)
No. Claire lives there, but not Mildred.

1. Does the Volkswagen need gas? (the Ford)
2. Do roses come out in April? (tulips)
3. Is Mrs. Stoll over forty years old? (Mrs. Stanhope)
4. Will Ruth be at the meeting? (Anna Mae)
5. Does she sew shirts? (dresses)
6. Does the zoo have a tiger? (a lion)
7. Is Greta wearing designer jeans? (regular blue jeans)
8. Does she want to plant flowers? (vegetables)
9. Did you cut your right hand? (my left hand)
10. Is it going to rain? (be cloudy)
11. Did the doctor give you vitamin E? (vitamin C)
12. Do the Boons have two daughters? (the Moseleys)
13. Was the program in the afternoon? (the morning and evening)

C. Study the picture. Form sentences about Jean and Jiro. Use **but** and a short clause.

Ex. Jiro doesn't take business, but Jean does.

109 Conjunctions: and vs. but

The vase fell **and** it broke.
The lamp fell **but** it didn't break.

A. Fill in the blanks with **and** or **but**.

1. The towels belong to Fred, __and__ the sweater does too.
2. Miss Teel went to Kancy College, _____ Mr. Seechrist did too.
3. Anne's children know Hindi, _____ Anne doesn't.
4. Harold won't stay at the dance, _____ Evelyn will.
5. I don't have skates, _____ neither does Russell.
6. Jackson didn't go to the hospital, _____ Bobby didn't either.
7. Fred doesn't have a sister, _____ Elvin does.
8. Bob doesn't know Marianna, _____ she doesn't know him.
9. The Bells left before seven, _____ so did the Alexanders.
10. The Giants wanted Dalin on their team, _____ the Indians kept him.

B. Form sentences like the example. Use **and** or **but** and a clause a–h.

1. Gilbert phoned his brother, _____.
2. Johnson bought those red pens, _____.
3. Stebbins left the game early, _____.
4. Phil played three games of chess with Jonathan, _____.
5. I passed the ball to Travis, _____.
6. Bill found Mary's textbook, _____.
7. Kemp paid the bill, _____.
8. I saw Bower in the hall, _____.

a. didn't give it to her.
b. didn't use them.
c. he fell down.
d. he wasn't home.
e. never went to that store again.
f. told him about you.
g. Warzicki came in.
h. won two.

C. Complete the sentences about each picture. Use **and** or **but** and a clause.

1. Harry looked in his pocket, **but he didn't find any money**.
2. Dorothy looked in her pocketbook, _____.
3. The snow got deep, _____.
4. Miss Wormley got in the tub, _____.
5. I looked for Hardwick's phone number, _____.
6. We put the milk in the refrigerator, _____.

110 Conjunctions: or

Did Wilson play in the game, **or** was he hurt?

A. Match 1–8 with a–h to form questions.

1. Did Amanda bring her lunch,
2. Did you fix the bike by yourself,
3. Did Mr. Bedford take the bus to work,
4. Do you want to play cards,
5. Is it going to rain,
6. Is the soccer ball outside,
7. Is a baby crying,
8. Will you be home at noon tomorrow,

a. or is a cat fighting over there?
b. or are you going to be out?
c. or did his wife drive him in the car?
d. or did he bring it in?
e. or did Edward help you?
f. or do you have to study now?
g. or is she going to a restaurant?
h. or will these clouds pass over?

B. Student 1: complete each question like the example. Use **or** and a verb from the list. Do not repeat the subject after **or**. Use a pronoun if necessary. Student 2: answer each question.

borrow	eat	lose
buy	forget	read
call	keep	rest
drive	laugh	walk

Ex. Did the Yankees win the game **or lose it？**
They lost.

1. Did you buy that book _____?
2. Did you grow these tomatoes _____?
3. Did the businessmen fly to New York _____?
4. Do you ride the bus to work _____?
5. Does the teacher remember the names _____?
6. Are you going to sell your old books _____?
7. Is Benny playing ball _____?
8. Were the children crying _____?
9. Were you taking a bath _____?
10. Was she working in the yard _____?
11. Will she write him a letter _____?

C. Form questions about each picture. Use **or** and a clause.

1. "Are you going to watch TV or go to bed now?"
   (or) "Do you want to go to bed now or watch this program?"

Teacher's Notes

The teacher may find that certain grammatical points require more than the one page of practice which each unit provides. It is suggested that drills and pictures from other units can be used. Only some of the many possibilities are cited below. Often, having the students identify and discuss ones that can and cannot be used is useful in itself. When using another picture, do not become involved with the grammar point of that unit, but simply interact with the picture. The teacher can also bring in magazine pictures to use with certain drills.

Unit 1 Other drills for this topic are 2A & B, 3A & B (use affirmative), 4A (use affirmative), 7A, 47A. PICTURES: Form sentences: 4, 5, 7, 56, 58, 60.

Unit 2 The present forms of *be* are not usually contracted in writing or in careful speech. In normal speech and informal writing *'m, 's, 're* are attached to the subject pronouns (Part A). Also, *'s* is attached to subject nouns except those ending with *ch, sh, ss, se, ce, ze, x*. In normal speech *is* and *are* are always reduced in pronunciation. Other drills for this topic are 5A, 1A & B, 8A (They were in the garage), 47. PICTURES: Form sentences: 58, 59, 60, 61.

Unit 3 Drills in Units 1, 2, 5, 7 can be adapted for this topic. PICTURES: 1 (The milk is not cold), 2 (She's not by the window), 5, 6, 7.

Unit 4 *N't* cannot be attached to the subject pronoun I. Other drills for this topic are in Units 1, 2, 3, 5, 7, 8. PICTURES: 1 (The milk is hot. It isn't cold), 2, 5, 6, 7.

Unit 5 Short answers to yes/no questions contain only three words: *Yes* + subject pronoun + a form of *be* (or *No* + pronoun with contracted *be* + *not*—or full form of *be* and *n't*). Form questions and answers with 4B (Are rocks hard? Yes, they are?), 7B (Is she fat? No, she isn't/she's not). PICTURES: Form questions & answers: 4, 7, 1, 2, 3.

Unit 6 *Is* can be contracted to *'s* and attached to question words. Drills 5A & B, 4B, 3B can be adapted; however items that have an adjective in the complement cannot be used because no question word is appropriate (5A #4, 6, 12). PICTURES: Form questions: 52, 56, 60, 64C, 72, 76, 13, 30, 31.

Unit 7 *Was* and *were* cannot be contracted with the subject. After doing Part A in the affirmative, go through it in the negative. Drills in Units 1–4 can be changed to past tense. PICTURES: 55 (The first day was cloudy. It wasn't sunny), 60, 72, 76, 1–4.

Unit 8 Drills 7A & B can be adapted, as well as drills in Units 1–6. As a variation, the drills in 8 can be adapted for question word questions: 8A (Where were they?), 8B (What was on sale?), 8C (Who was a good boy?).

Unit 9 The pronunciation of the verb *-s* form is regular except for *is, has, does, says*. Part A has one verb ending with each consonant sound. For more practice, use the verbs in Unit 20. Also, the sentences in these drills that have singular subjects can be used: 24A, 26A (use only sentences that make sense in habitual meaning).

Unit 10 This unit contrasts the plain verb form with the -s form. Drills in Units 11 and 12 can be adapted. Also use sentences from Units 23–26 that make sense in habitual present. PICTURES: Form sentences: 66, 67, 73A, 74.

Unit 11 Vary the drills by using the uncontracted negative word *not*, which is more careful and formal usage. Drills 9B and 10A & B can be used for extension—in 10A *always* comes after the auxiliary (don't always leave). PICTURES: Form sentences: 46 (doesn't have), 65, 69, 73A.

Unit 12 In Part B either a Yes or No answer can be given. For extension, drills in Units 10 and 11 can be adapted. PICTURES: Form questions: 10, 11, 13, 104, 106, 108.

Unit 13 For extension use sentences in Unit 28 that make sense in present tense. Also, teacher can give verbs from Unit 9 as cues; student 1 forms any question word question and student 2 answers. PICTURES: Form questions: 10, 11, 13, 104, 106, 108. Note that sometimes the simple present is used for future scheduled action (13C#1). In many cases it is also present because it happens regularly (every day) at the same time (13A#1, 4; B#6, 7).

Unit 14 Practice the full form of the auxiliary *be* in Part A and the contracted or reduced pronunciation in B. For more practice use contractions in A and full forms in B. PICTURES: Use the ones that work in Units 48 (#2: She's looking for a clean uniform), 50, 59, 62, 64, 65, 66, 67, 70, 72.

Unit 15 Vary the exercises by using the uncontracted negative word *not* with the contractions of *be* (He's not eating rice). Then use the full forms without contractions, which is more careful and formal usage (He is not eating rice.). Drills in 14 and 29 can be adapted. PICTURES: Form negative sentences: 59 (He isn't studying/working now), 69, 72, 77, 10.

Unit 16 For more practice with negative short answers do Part A (No, he isn't). Also, 30A & B can be adapted. For more creative practice, provide a list of verbs that can be used in questions pertaining to the students and have students create and answer the questions. PICTURES: 14 (Is the woman filling the glasses/drinking?), 15, 30.

Unit 17 In Part A use the continuous with all time expressions that include the present moment. A frequency word (like *often*, Part B) requires simple present. PICTURE: Form sentences: 66 (He's spilling his soup. He always spills it), 10, 13.

Unit 18 The verbs *smell, taste, feel* have three uses: He's smelling the food (actively); He smells the food (passively notices the smell); It smells good (linking verb). For the senses of hearing and sight there are three different verbs for these uses: listen to, hear, sound; look at (or watch), see, look.

Unit 19 The present continuous can also be used for future action that is expected to happen (Part A example, B#1). In many cases it is hard to tell out of context whether the meaning is present or future (C#1). For more work, use items from Unit 13 that make sense in the continuous. Also, two students form and answer question word questions about sentences in 14B (Where's it raining? In St. Louis), 15B, 16B, 17B. PICTURES: Form questions: 15, 16, 17, 65, 66, 69, 70, 71.

Unit 20 The three pronunciations of the

regular past tense suffix are /ɪd/, /t/, /d/. Part A has final vowels or single final consonants; B has final clusters. Unit 9 can be done in past tense.

Unit 21 Only regular verbs are included. Vary Part A by providing the negative sentence and having students form the affirmative, which will have the past form of the verb. PICTURES: Form sentences: 10, 12, 14, 15.

Unit 22 Only regular verbs are included. Use the items in 21A for additional practice. PICTURES: Form questions: 16, 22, 71, 72, 8.

Unit 23 These verbs have no change in past tense (cut) or have a /d/ suffix with a stem change (sold). Part A has yes/no questions; B has question word questions; all three have affirmative statements. Part A can be varied to have negative statements (I didn't cut my arm; I cut my finger). Additional items for A: have/good luck//bad luck; say/thank you//I'm sorry; put away/ toys//clothes.

Unit 24 These verbs have a /t/ suffix with a stem change in past tense. (*Go* and *went* actually have completely different stems.) Change Part B to use question word questions: 1 What (What did you buy? I bought a new bike), 2 When, 3 What, 4 How much, 5 What language, 6 What, 7 Which bus, 8 When.

Unit 25 These verbs have a vowel change in past tense: take, begin, forget, speak, read, win, meet, drink, find, sing, get, give, eat, wear, wake, ring. More items for Part A: begin/at 9:00//at 9:30; eat/ at a restaurant//at home; wear/jeans// a suit; forget/his comb//his wallet; wake up/in time//late; ring/the right doorbell//the wrong one. The reading in B has two structures that may need to be explained to students: verb + infinitive (began to read), verb + noun clause (don't think I slept). Students can ask and answer yes/no questions about the story in B (Did John's roommate meet him at the door? Yes, he did).

Unit 26 These verbs have a vowel change in the past tense. The verbs include those listed at the beginning of Part A plus *break, come, drive, write*. Students can ask and answer *when* questions in Part C (When did you draw it? I drew it several years ago).

Unit 27 Units 9–12 have a mixture of regular and irregular verbs that can be adapted to past tense. PICTURES: Form sentences or questions: 10, 12, 50, 59, 61, 62, 63, 65, 66, 67, 69.

Unit 28 Includes both regular and irregular verbs. Unit 13 can be adapted for past tense (except B#4, C#1). PICTURES: Form questions: 10, 12, 50, 59, 62, 65, 66, 67, 69, 32.

Unit 29 Units 14 and 15 can be adapted to past continuous. PICTURES: Form sentences: 14, 15, 16, 19–22.

Unit 30 Part B can be varied by letting students change the object or place adverb (Was M helping her sister?). Drills in Units 14, 15, 29 can be adapted. PICTURES: Form questions: 14, 15, 16, 29.

Unit 31 Some of the verbs avoid the continuous (*saw* in A#1); in other cases the meaning determines if the verb is continuous or not (*met* in A#2 is a nondurative action).

Unit 32 In informal speech *going to* is pronounced "gonna." Students should learn this for aural recognition but do not need to produce it themselves. As a variant, students can use different sentence subjects for Part B (#1: Is his sister going to get well? Omit #5). Drills in Units 34, 27, 21 can be adapted. PICTURES: Form sentences: 57, 61, 62, 65, 69, 77, 19, 20, 21.

Unit 33 Drills in Units 35, 28, 22 can be adapted. Vary some drills by using question word questions: 33A (When are you going to paint the garage? What are you going to paint? Who's going to paint the garage?), 33B (Where are those birds going to go?).

Unit 34 In speech *will* is contracted to *'ll* and attached to subject pronouns and nouns. Drills in Units 32, 27, 21 can be adapted. PICTURES: Form sentences about the action in the picture or about a consequence or what is in the picture: 54 (It won't rain today. We'll have a picnic; or, It'll be a nice day tomorrow), 61, 63, 70, 71, 10, 11, 16, 29, 32. For special practice with the verb *be*: 2A (She'll be in this room), 3A, 4A. Also, use items from these drills that make sense in future: 1B, 2B, 3B, 4B.

Unit 35 Drills in Units 33, 28, 22 can be adapted. PICTURES: 63, 70, 10, 13, 28, 33. Also practice with the verb *be* 5A (Will he be a mechanic?).

Unit 36 This unit includes *be going to* and *will* futures. *Will* and *going to* can be exchanged in Parts A and B for more practice. As a variant, students can make up their own answers for A (#1: You'll see me next week). Drills in Units 32–35 can be adapted. PICTURES: Form questions: 32, 34, 35, 86, 92.

Unit 37 This unit includes four ways to express future: *going to, will,* present continuous, simple present. As a variant, students can make up answers for Part B (#1: No, I'll take Italian). Additional items for short responses: Are you going to watch the new TV program tonight? Will Mr. Eden be home early tonight? Will you be home all day tomorrow? Do the Eagles play the Giants tomorrow? Will Tommy get a haircut today? Are you having lunch with Mr. Grant today?

Unit 38 Students should learn the reduced pronunciation of *can* for aural recognition and for production themselves because the stress is an important distinguishing factor between *can* and *can't*. As a variant, students can change the words after the verb in Part B (Can you see the door?). PICTURES: Form sentences: 11.

Unit 39 Students should learn the colloquial pronunciations "hasta," "hafta," "wanna" for aural recognition. They do not need to produce these themselves. As a variant, students can change the words after the verb in Part B (Do you want to take a picture of that?). Also, B can be varied for question word questions (What do you want to take? A bath). PICTURES: Use *have to* or *want to* as appropriate with various pictures: 71 (#1: He has to wipe up the water), 72, 16.

Unit 40 The four inflected forms of the verb are: plain (no ending), -s form, -ing form, past tense form.

Unit 41 The negative word *not(n't)* always comes after an auxiliary. Some sentences of Drill 40C make sense if changed to negative. Drills in 42, 80–84 can be adapted. PICTURES: Use various tenses: 80 (They're cooking fish. They aren't cooking meat), 81, 83, 13, 20.

Unit 42 Unit 41 can be adapted for additional practice (A. Does Al drive a truck? No he doesn't; B. Are the traffic lights working? No, they aren't). PICTURES: Form questions: 41, 80, 84, 65, 71.

Unit 43 The main grammatical uses of nouns are sentence subject, complement of the verb *be*, object of a verb, and object of a preposition. These uses can be identified in other sentences, for example, drills 50B, 46B. PICTURES: Form sentences about the pictures in these units using a singular noun as sentence subject and as object of a place preposition: 60 (A nurse is in the room), 76, 78.

Unit 44 The plural suffix has three possible pronunciations: /z/, /s/, /ɪz/. For more practice pluralize the countable nouns in Unit 43 (roses—but not bread). PICTURES: Form plural nouns about things in the pictures of other units: 72 (windows), 75, 2.

Unit 45 The types of irregularity are vowel change (feet), vowel change and unusual ending (children), voicing of the final consonant + suffix /z/ (wives, paths). Some other words of these types are oxen, brethren, moose, salmon, houses, calves, hooves, scarves, baths, youths, oaths, wreaths, truths.

Unit 46 Certain noun determiners can precede plural nouns, others precede singular nouns, and others both. Additional items for Part C: 1/pocket (kangaroo), 3/feet (yardstick), 6/legs (insect), 64/squares (checkerboard).

Unit 47 Certain types of nouns are often noncountable: substances, liquids, abstract qualities. The unit can be extended by practicing nouns that can have both countable and noncountable uses: cake, paper, string, film, candy. Also practice noncountable nouns in an *of* phrase after individualizers (a piece/drop of . . .), units of measure (a pound/yard/quart of . . .), containers (a box/bottle of . . .). Parts A and B can be adapted if students have been introduced to *how much* and *how many*; use verbs *want, need, buy*: How many balloons do you want? PICTURES: The classifiers (a bag of) are also used with plural nouns. Form noun phrases with noncountable and plural nouns in these pictures: 68 (a bag of potatoes), 74, 99.

Unit 48 No possessive suffix is added to an -s plural suffix, except the apostrophe in writing. Part B has plural possessives. Unit 53 also deals with possessives. Students can explain the meaning relationship of the possessive in each phrase: ownership (Jake's bike), partitive (bear's ears), personal relationship (my uncle). Form additional noun phrases using the possessive nouns in A and B and adding different head nouns (a bear's life). Form noun phrases with two possessives by using names 8–14 in A and adding another possessive (Butch's brother's lunch). PICTURES: Form noun phrases about things that you see in other pictures: 36 (bear's fur), 61, 62, 63, 71, 80.

Unit 49 The four forms of the noun are summarized. In speech, regular nouns have only two forms, since the plural, possessive, and plural possessive are all pronounced the same. For more practice, students can form phrases or sentences about classroom objects or other students' belongings (Betty's pen/flowers).

Unit 50 Words beginning with most of the letters of the alphabet are in Part A; these words can be used for additional sounds: apron, city, automobile, chair, evening, giant, inch, theater, ocean, whale, oil can, xylophone, ounce. Do A again, inserting suitable adjectives from B (That looks like a strange lake). PICTURES: Form noun phrases for things you see in these pictures: 63, 76, 93, 97, 101 (the *an* words are: 63 exam, "A"; 76 office; 93 auto, accident, officer; 97 airplane; 101 apartment, office, ice cream).

Unit 51 In Part A *the* is used with nouns that have only one definite reference in any given situation. In B *the* is used when certain adjectives are present (superlatives, *only*, etc.). In C *the* is used with a noun whose definite reference was established in the preceding sentence, i.e., the question (a page—the page). For other practice use *the* instead of *a/an* in 50A; pronounce it /ðiy/ or /ðə/.

Unit 52 In Part A the definite reference is established in the preceding sentence (a lamp—the switch). In C *the* is used when only one is present (the raincoat); *a/an* when more than one (an umbrella).

Unit 53 In compound possessives (Part B) either *Ray's and Ruth's* or *Ray and Ruth's* is correct. Unit 48 has more practice on possessive noun modifiers only. Unit 90 also practices possessives. PICTURES: Form questions about 82 (Is the wallet Christine's father's present? No, it's her mother's), 108 (Is that Jean's science book? No, it's Jiro's).

Unit 54 For more practice use appropriate adjectives and *one/ones* in Part A (No. He has an old one). PICTURES: Ask questions about things in various pictures; use a common adjective that will produce a *no* answer: 77 (Is she an old nurse? No, a young one), 60, 4. Also, *what kind of* questions can be asked: What kind of nurse is she? A good one.

Unit 55 Ordinals are formed by adding -th to the cardinal numbers (fourth) except for *first, second, third, next, last*. (Note that *last* can mean "the previous one" [opposite of *next*] or "the final one" [opposite of *first*].) For more practice ask and answer questions about the map in Unit 31 (What's their fourth stop? They're in Denver—what was their last stop?).

Unit 56 In Part B the distinction between *this/these* for near objects and *that/those* for far objects is made automatically; the words *that* and *those* receive loud stress for emphatic contrast. PICTURES in Units 58 and 106 can be adapted (This bottle is full. Those are empty).

Unit 57 The indefinites (*other, another*) can refer to something additional or to something different. Let students identify which meaning is present in each sentence of Part B. PICTURES in 45, 82, 90 (One student is fat; the other is thin), 108 can be adapted.

Unit 58 In Part A, cardinal numbers are used as noun substitutes (in Example A, *Two* substitutes for *Two girls*). The word *one* is optional after *another* or *other*; some speakers prefer not to use *ones*. Students may identify the "additional" or "different" meaning of the indefinites in B. PICTURES: Form sentences with 30 (One city is getting rain, the other isn't), 32, 90.

Unit 59 First and second person pronouns are in Part A; third person ones in B. For more practice change subject nouns to pronouns in sentences of other drills: 45B, 49C, 57A. PICTURES: Ask a question and have students answer with a pronoun: 11 (What's the boy doing? He's swimming), 6 (Where's the cake? It's on the table), 19, 20, 21, 32.

Unit 60 For more practice change object nouns to pronouns in sentences of other drills (only nouns with definite determiners): 90B. Substitute in these sentences the items which are given for 10A (*He* was there. The police saw *him*). PICTURES: Ask "Do you see the _____?" Student answers with a pronoun, "Yes, I see it/them," etc. Use various pictures throughout the book.

Unit 61 These are sometimes called possessive adjectives. Drill 62A can be adapted (Then it's her pin. Then it's your ring). PICTURES: Form sentences with 19 (Their furniture is in the truck), 11, 82, 87, 90.

Unit 62 PICTURES: 29 (Is that Billy's bike? Yes, it's his), 82, 106, 108.

Unit 63 A preposition can sometimes be omitted before a reflexive pronoun with no difference in meaning: Part B#1 Ken opened the can (by) himself; #10 I kept the valuable ones (for) myself. PICTURES: Form sentences using these verbs: enjoy, hurt, make, buy, tire out, be mad at: 48 (He is/isn't enjoying himself), 59, 71, 21, 23 (#1, 2), 24 (#3).

Unit 64 Additional items for Part A: Jim wrote to Ann . . . , Betty asked about Tom. . . . , Joe was looking at Cindy . . . , Janet was depending on Fred. . . . PICTURES: Form sentences; use pronouns: 48 (He got them dirty/He has chalk on them), 50, 59, 65.

Unit 65 Affirmative statements use *some*, negative statements use *any*, yes/no questions use either but using *some* shows that the speaker expects a yes answer and *any* expects a no answer. Add to Part B: pennies, change, writing paper, spoons, tape, batteries, toast. PICTURES: Ask questions with some or any: 44 (Does he have any tickets?), 52, 54, 58, 68, 7 (Do you see any animals in the picture?), 72, 77, 2.

Unit 66 Adapt 47B (Did M want some beans? No, he didn't want any. Did M want a vegetable? No, he didn't want one). PICTURES: Form sentences: 52 (The picture has a raincoat/some umbrellas in it), 54, 58, 60.

Unit 67 Vary B; use *much* or *many* in questions (Do you drink much coffee?). Adapt 47B (Did M want many beans? No, he didn't want many. Did M want much bread? No, he didn't want much). PICTURES: Form sentences: 52 (The closet doesn't have many raincoats in it), 66, 70, 71, 73A.

Unit 68 Sometimes *many* and *much* are interchangeable with *a lot (of)*, but often there is a negative implication *many* and *much* in negative statements and in yes/no questions (not many beans = few beans; not much bread = little bread; not a lot of beans/bread = a few beans/a little bread). Adapt the drills of Unit 66: A. Substitute *a lot of*, *a*, or *an*; B. Fill in *many, much, a lot of, a, an* or *one*; C. Use *many, much,* or *a lot of* as modifiers. PICTURES: Form sentences: 44 (He doesn't have many tickets), 52, 54.

Unit 69 Adapt drills in Unit 67: A. Use a *few* or a *little* in an affirmative sentence (I have a few pens), B. (Do you drink coffee? Yes, but only a little), C. use *a few* or *a little* (They only took a few suitcases). PICTURES: Form sentences: 66, 1.

Unit 70 Adapt Part A in Unit 68; use *few, little,* or *a lot of* (He bought few potatoes). PICTURES: Form sentences: 8 (omit #1), 41, 102.

Unit 71 Quantifiers can precede *of* and a definite modifier. When the noun phrase is used as sentence subject, the verb agrees in number with the quantifier, not the definite *of* phrase (Part C #11, 12). Adapt 69B (A little of it did), 67B (Yes, but not much of it), 66A (She bought some of the socks), 65A (We need some of that sugar, but we don't need any of the pepper). PICTURES: Form sentences: 65, 66, 73A, 35, 41, 79, 94.

Unit 72 *Both* and *each* refer to two; *all* and *every* refer to more than two (*Each* can also refer to more than two). After *all* and *both*, *of* is optional before a definite modifier (Part A) but is necessary before a personal pronoun (Part B). Adapt 71C: Fill in *both of, all of, each (one) of,* or *every one of*. In 69B use *All of it/them* or *Every one of them*. PICTURES: Form sentences: 85, 90, 105, 108, 110.

Unit 73 After *half*, *of* is optional before a definite modifier but is necessary before a personal pronoun. Adapt 71C; use an ordinal number (omit #11, 12). PICTURES: Form sentences: 89, 105.

Unit 74 Some modifiers can modify countable nouns, some can modify uncountable nouns, and some can modify both (Part A). Part B contrasts definite modifiers with indefinite quantifying modifiers. PICTURES: Form sentences: 86, 88, 99.

Unit 75 Two sentences in Part A have structures that may need to be explained to students: #8 has an indefinite pronoun + infinitive, #15 has a noun clause complement after *feel*. As a variation, give A without providing the choices that are in parentheses.

Unit 76 It is courteous to place *I* (or *me*) second in a compound noun phrase. Vary Parts A and B by adding another noun to form compounds that contain three nouns. Use series intonation when speaking such a compound (Dick, Jane, and I saw a dog in the garage. He ate cereal, fruit, and toast for breakfast). PICTURES: Form sentences: 50 (He hurt an arm and a leg), 52, 55, 58, 60, 68, 69, 72, 73.

Unit 77 Use the correct intonation for alternative questions—rising then falling. Vary the drills by adding another noun to form phrases that contain three nouns (A. Did M tell her friend, her mother, or Mr. Lamb? B. Do you want a hot dog, a hamburger, or a sandwich? C. Are the flowers on a table, a bench, or the floor?). PICTURES: Form alternative questions about the pictures: 48 (Does he have ink or chalk on his hands?), 51, 55, 56, 57.

Unit 78 The verb *be* is followed by a noun, adjective, or adverb as a complement. The adverb is usually one of location, but with an event noun as sentence subject it may be a time adverb (Part B #3,4). For more practice see 43A, 47A, 53B & C, 56B and Units 1–8. PICTURES: Form sentences: 43, 1–8.

Unit 79 Most linking verbs refer to the senses or indicate a state or changing condition (become). The complement is usually an adjective—occasionally a noun (Part B #i) or a *like* phrase (A #10,12; B #m). Students can look for sentences that make sense with the verb *be* changed to a linking verb in Units 1–10, 78.

Unit 80 As a variant, students can change the direct object in Parts A (Do rabbits eat candy?) and B (She is teaching science). Or, they can change the verb (A. Do horses eat meat? B. She is learning arithmetic). Many verbs in Unit 81 can take a direct object; add objects where possible.

Unit 81 Drop the object from sentences in Unit 80 where possible (Do rabbits eat? Yes, they do). Identify verbs in Units 9–27 that can be used without a direct object.

Unit 82 As a variant students can change the indirect object (Mr. S wrote Mr. T a letter). Also, the indirect object nouns can be changed to pronouns (Mr. S wrote them a letter). For more practice use the drills in Unit 83, but do not use a pronoun for the direct object (Josh got her the ticket).

Unit 83 The *to* and *for* version is preferred when the direct object is a personal pronoun. In A use a pronoun direct object. Also, use drills in 82 (Mr. S wrote a letter to the company).

Unit 84 Students can fill in *be* or another verb in a drill that has a series of sentences; use 49B & C by striking out the verbs that are in them. (Also 50B, 51A, 54B, 55A, 57A, 59B).

Unit 85 *There* sentences tell the existence of something in a place and/or time. If no place or time expres-

114 TEACHER'S NOTES

sion is present, the sentence must refer to a place or time that is obvious from context or else it refers to any place or all time. For more practice form sentences with 78B using adverbs i–p (There's a crow on the roof). Use pictures elsewhere in the book (43B: There's a bear in the tent).

Unit 86 Two students form yes/no questions and short answers using items in Unit 85 (Is there sugar on the cake? Yes, there is/No, there isn't). Use pictures elsewhere in the book (43B: Is there a dog in the tent? No, there isn't).

Unit 87 The verb is usually singular after *what* and *who* even if it's obvious to the speaker that the answer is plural (B#11: Who goes to medical school? Doctors do). For more practice, two students ask and answer questions based on sentences elsewhere in the book: 27A(Who went to school? Ned did), 28B, 4B, 14B. Also, use other pictures: 43(What's in the tent?), 29(Who was studying?).

Unit 88 As a variant, students can change the verb in Part B (N paid for the curtains). For more practice two students ask and answer questions based on sentences elsewhere in the book: 21A (What did B study last night? English), 23B, 24A, 10B. PICTURES: 65, 66, 17, 18.

Unit 89 *Which* can be used as a modifier before a noun (*which knife*), a modifier before the substitute word *one/s* (*which one/s*), or as a substitute itself (*which*). Form questions using *which* + noun as subject based on Part B (Which boy took a dessert?). For more practice ask *which* questions about sentence #1, 3, 4, 5, 8, 12 in 71B (Which ones did it lose?).

Unit 90 *Whose* can be used as a modifier before a noun (*whose knife*) or as a substitute (*whose*). It can refer to a subject, object of verb, or object of preposition—see examples at top of Unit 90 page. Use drills in Units 61 (Whose grandfather is Mr. Hayes?), 53, 62. PICTURES: Form sentences: 61, 62, 19, 29.

Unit 91 For more practice use 42B (Where are the hockey games?), 102B. PICTURES: 85 (Where's the blood?), 56, 102, 104. Use the determiner *what* in asking location: 91B (What [kind of] place does Jason eat lunch at? The sandwich shop. What city was Miss A in? Hong Kong). Also 102A (What street did he live on? Joliet Street).

Unit 92 Part B in Unit 103 can be adapted (When will he come? On Sunday). PICTURES: Form questions: 10, 13(#1,2), 28(omit #2,3), 31, 92.

Unit 93 Various pictures throughout the book can be used to practice questions about quantity: 43B (How many bears are in the tent/in the picture? Only one. How much tea spilled? One cup), 45, 52, 58. Also, drills in Unit 65 can be adapted (A. How much salad do you need? B. Do you want some dessert? Yes, please. How much do you want? Just a little, please).

Unit 94 Form questions using other drills that have series of sentences: 32B (What's E going to do? Who's going to skate? What are you going to eat?), 25B, 72B, 63B. PICTURES: Ask one question using each question word at the top of Unit 94 (if possible) about each picture: 43, 60, 64, 72, 76, 77, 3, 7, 78.

Unit 95 In speech there are two intonation patterns for tag questions. Rising intonation on the tag indicates that the speaker is suggesting the answer but wants the respondent to give his answer. Falling intonation indicates that the answer is expected to agree with the question. Practice these drills using each intonation in turn. For more practice use drills in 1–4, 7, 78. PICTURES: 43, 31, 79, 90.

Unit 96 Drills in Units 14, 15, 29 can be adapted. PICTURES: 60, 64, 15, 16, 80, 81.

Unit 97 Drills in Units 10, 11, 21, 23–27, 80–83 can be adapted. PICTURES: Form questions: 20, 21, 11, 78.

Unit 98 Drills in Unit 85 can be adapted (A. There's sugar on the cake, isn't there?). PICTURES: Use various tenses: 43 (There's a bear in the tent, isn't there?), 60, 72, 2, 7.

Unit 99 Change Part A using different tenses from those given (Ralph liked kites, didn't he? He isn't going to have any kites from S, is he?). Other drills can be adapted: 84A (The Ortegas aren't Mexicans, are they?), 57A, 66B, 75A.

Unit 100 Negative yes/no questions can be used when the answer is expected to agree with the question, or as in Part C when the speaker thinks that the answer should be yes. For more practice adapt drills in Units 95 and 85. PICTURES: 43 (Isn't that a bear in the tent?), 33, 56, 58, 59, 63.

Unit 101 Part C includes both *do* and *be* auxiliaries. For more practice two students can use any of several picture drills in the book. One student makes a statement about the picture and the other responds with a negative question indicating something he thinks should be true. Use units 84, 79, 80, 81 (*be* and *do* can be included).

Unit 102 This unit has the basic prepositions of place and direction. Additional items for Part A: New City, a new house, 412 Oak Street, Vermont (a state), the Netherlands, the next block. Drill 91B can be adapted: fill in prepositions *in*, *on*, *at*, *to*. Also, the words *out*, *off*, *away*, *in*, *on*, *there* can be used alone as adverbs. In various drills change the place expression or add one: 26A (He sat on the floor), 28A (I taught chemistry in high school).

Unit 103 Add to Part A: yesterday afternoon, tomorrow evening, last evening. Parts B and C in Unit 92 can be used. PICTURES: Form sentences: 10, 31, 33, 42.

Unit 104 Usually place is before time. Add time expressions in Unit 91 and add place expressions in 92. Add place and time expressions in sentences in 17B, 29B, 33B, 79B. PICTURES: Form sentences: 28, 31, 92, 98.

Unit 105 Vary Part B by forming a yes/no question (Are they ever/sometimes/often wrong about the weather?). Add appropriate frequency expressions to sentences in Units 1–13, 21–28, 32–39. Some sentences will not permit any frequency word. Some sentences already have a frequency word, but a different one may also be appropriate.

Unit 106 For further practice adapt these: 87B (J brought the salad, and H brought the cake), 88B (N made the curtains, and P made the doll), 47A (Balloons are round, and pencils are long). Students may create a clause after *and*: 6B (AJ is my brother's wife, and JJ is his sister). PICTURES: 28 (They ran to the gate and saw the plane take off), 78, 91, 93.

Unit 107 For extension use 52A (I bought a lamp, but the switch was broken), 13B (G lives in New Orleans, but P lives in St. Louis), 41A (Al drives a truck, but Art drives a car), 57A, 21A. PICTURES: Form sentences: 56, 57, 58, 62, 64, 70, 30, 32, 35, 38. Students may discuss the reasons for using *but*; in the example for 107B the speaker may be looking for a person who is both Spanish and from Madrid.

Unit 108 For more practice use 12B (No, they don't speak English, but Enrico does), 29B (R wasn't earning $1200, but $1400 [#6–11 must use a verb in the short clause]), 57A (J is tall, but the other men aren't).

Unit 109 For more practice use the first clause of sentences in 56A and let students make up an *and* or *but* clause (I like this necktie, but I'm not going to buy it/and I'm going to keep it), 50B (We had a lesson today, and it was easy/but it was hard). Also add clauses to 70B, 24A, 1B, 3B. Drill 5B can be done with short clauses (B's tired and M is too. I'm afraid, but you aren't).

Unit 110 All sentences are alternative questions. Drills can be statements using *either . . . or* (A. A either brought her lunch, or she's going to a restaurant. B. The Yankees either won the game or lost it). For more practice use 11B (Do fish fly or [do they] swim?), 32B (Is E going to play or [is she going to] work?), 34B, 38A.

Answer Key

Unit 1 A: 1. You are warm. 2. I am warm. 3. is 4. are 5. is 6. are 7. is 8. are 9. are 10. is 11. is 12. are **B:** 2. are 3. is 4. are 5. am 6. are 7. is 8. are 9. are 10. am 11. are 12. is 13. are 14. are 15. are **C:** 2. The kittens are hungry. 3. Their feet are dirty. 4. Mrs. Winter is angry.

Unit 2 A: 1. He's in this room. 2. He's on the phone. 3. You're on the phone. 4. You're by the door. 5. I'm by the door. 6. It's by the door. 7. It's in the box. 8. They're in the box. 9. They're very nice. 10. She's very nice. 11. She's a pilot. 12. I'm a pilot. 13. I'm ready now. **B:** 3. elephant's 4. What's 5. college is 6. class is 7. Who's 8. Where's 9. ride's 10. house is 11. garden's 12. A vase is **C:** 2. What's, Some flowers. 3. Where's (Where are), They're on her desk. 4. Where are, They're on her desk. 5. What's, A typewriter. 6. What's, Some flowers.

Unit 3 A: 1. You're not right. 2. You're not in the right place. 3. It's not in the right place. 4. We're not in the right place. 5. She's not in the right place. 6. She's not a good swimmer. 7. I'm not a good swimmer. 8. He's not a good swimmer. 9. You're not a good swimmer. 10. You're not good swimmers. 11. They're not good swimmers. 12. They're not ready. **B:** 2. is not 3. is not 4. are not 5. is not 6. are not 7. is not 8. are not 9. is not 10. are not 11. are not 12. are not **C:** 2. 's not open. It's 3. are not in the taxicab/trunk. They're 4. are not off. They're 5. 's not the (taxi) driver. She's

Unit 4 A: 1. The theater isn't full. 2. The trash cans aren't full. 3. isn't 4. isn't 5. aren't 6. isn't 7. aren't 8. aren't 9. isn't 10. isn't 11. aren't 12. isn't **B:** 2. It isn't 3. He isn't 4. They aren't 5. It isn't 6. They're aren't 7. She isn't 8. They aren't 9. It isn't 10. They aren't 11. It isn't 12. They aren't **C:** 2. aren't open. They're closed 3. isn't quiet. It's noisy 4. isn't single. He's married 5. isn't sweet. It's sour 6. isn't quick. It's slow 7. isn't slow. It's quick.

Unit 5 A: 1. Is Mary in the garage? Yes, she is. (No, she isn't.) 2. Are the tools in the garage? Yes, they are. (No, they aren't.) 3. Is Bill in the garage? Yes, he is. 4. Is Bill hungry? Yes, he is. 5. Are they hungry? Yes, they are. 6. Are they tired? Yes, they are. 7. Are you tired? Yes, we are. 8. Is the teacher tired? Yes, he/she is. 9. Is your friend tired? Yes, he/she is. 10. Is your friend in the hospital? Yes, he/she is. 11. Is your friend on the second floor? Yes, he/she is. 12. Is your friend all right? Yes, he/she is. **B:** 1. Are you afraid? No, I'm not. 2. Is your watch wrong? No, it isn't. 3. Are her eyes brown? Yes, they are. 4. Are the tools in the garage? Yes, they are. 5. Are the cookies in the oven? No, they aren't. 6. Is Bill at the hospital? Yes, he is. 7. Is the typist out of white paper? No, she/he isn't. 8. Are Mr. and Mrs. Young here? Yes, they are. 9. Am I in the front row? No, you aren't. 10. Is that a cheese sandwich? Yes, it is. **C:** Suggested answers: 2. Is that boy hungry/thirsty? Yes, he is. 3. Is Jenny tired? No, she isn't. 4. Are those books heavy? Yes, they are.

Unit 6 A: 2. When are 3. Who's 4. Who are 5. Where are 6. When's 7. What are 8. Who's 9. What are 10. Where's **B:** 1. When's the election of officers? Today. 2. What are sharks? Fish. 3. What's Martha's car? A Ford. 4. When are his brothers' birthdays? In the summer. 5. What's in the refrigerator? The vegetables. 6. Where's the railroad station? On Q Street. 7. Who's the president? Terry Jones. **C:** Suggested answers: 2. Where's the English 2 class? In Room 206. 3. When's lunch? At 12 o'clock. 4. What's in his pocket? A pen. 5. What's in that truck? Bread.

Unit 7 A: 1. Some glasses were in the kitchen. 2. We were in the kitchen. 3. were 4. was 5. was 6. was 7. were 8. was 9. were 10. was 11. were 12. was. **B:** 1. We weren't interested. We were bored. 2. He wasn't young. He was old. 3. weren't . . . were 4. weren't . . . were 5. wasn't . . . was 6. wasn't . . . He was 7. wasn't . . . She was 8. wasn't . . . It was 9. Weren't . . . We were 10. wasn't . . . She was 11. wasn't . . . He was **C:** Suggested answers: 2. The windows weren't closed. 3. The key was in the door. 4. Mrs. Kinkaid wasn't home. 5. The door was open. 6. The piano was by the window.

Unit 8 A: 1. Was she the receptionist? Yes, she was. (or No, she wasn't. 2. Were we in the right building? Yes, we/you were. (or No, we/you weren't. 3. Was I . . . Yes, you were. 4. Were you . . . Yes, we were. 5. Was it . . . Yes, it was. 6. Were . . . Yes, they were. 7. Were . . . Yes, they were. 8. Were . . . Yes, they were. 9. Was . . . Yes, she was. 10. Was . . . Yes, he was. 11. Were . . . Yes we were. **B:** Suggested answers: 2. Was the child lonesome? No, he/she wasn't. 3. Were the cups with the saucers? Yes, they were. 4. Were the doors shut? No, they weren't. 5. Was the front like the back? Yes, it was. 6. Was the game exciting? No, it wasn't. 7. Were the islands near the coast? Yes, they were. 8. Was January a warm month? No, it wasn't. 9. Was your office above the classroom? Yes, it was. 10. Were the ropes strong? No, they weren't. 11. Were the toys for little children? Yes, they were. 12. Were you and Al together? No, we weren't. **C:** Suggested answers: 2. Were many people in the audience? No, few were. 3. Were the apples green? Yes, they were. 4. Were the brakes good? No, they weren't.

Unit 9 A: /z/: 2. feels 3. gives 4. hears 6.

knows 9. needs 13. rings 14. robs 15. runs 16. seems 18. tries; /s/: 7. laughs 8. looks 11. puts 17. stops; /ɪz/: 5. judges 10. passes 12. reaches 19. wishes **B:** 2. helps /s/ 3. fixes /ɪz/ 4. marches /ɪz/ 5. burns /z/ 6. holds /z/ 7. asks /s/ 8. parks /s/ 9. wants /s/ 10. turns /z/ 11. lasts /s/ 12. charges /ɪz/ 13. sounds /z/ 14. dances /ɪz/

Unit 10 A: 1. The bus always leaves at one o'clock. 2. We always leave at one o'clock. 3. leaves 4. leave 5. leaves 6. leave 7. leaves 8. leave 9. leaves 10. leave 11. leaves 12. leaves **B:** 2. falls 3. come 4. uses/takes 5. taste 6. sits 7. ask 8. earn 9. speaks 10. takes 11. drink 12. crosses **C:** Suggested answers: 2. She takes a shower at 7:15. 3. She eats breakfast at 7:45. 4. She gets on the bus at eight o'clock. 5. She gets to work at 8:30. 6. She eats/has lunch at noon.

Unit 11 A: 1. Mary doesn't look bad. 2. You don't look bad. 3. don't sound 4. doesn't sound 5. don't sound 6. don't feel 7. don't feel 8. don't feel 9. don't smell 10. doesn't smell 11. doesn't taste 12. doesn't taste **B:** 2. doesn't write 3. don't live 4. doesn't set 5. don't feel 6. doesn't rain 7. don't cost 8. doesn't have 9. don't open 10. doesn't begin 11. don't use 12. doesn't equal **C:** 2. The man doesn't have any money. 3. The man doesn't understand English. 4. The man doesn't drive (to work).

Unit 12 A: 1. Do/hurt//they don't 2. Does/look (seem)//it doesn't 3. Does/stop//it does 4. Do/have (need)//they do 5. Does/like//he does 6. Do/seem//they don't 7. Do/use (need, have, make)//I do 8. Do/need (have)//you don't 9. Does/eat (have)//she does 10. Does/look//it doesn't 11. Do/live//they don't **B:** 1. Yes, it does. (No, it doesn't.) Does it rain here during the winter? No, it doesn't. (Yes, it does.) 2. Yes, I do. Does Miss Long cook with butter? No, she doesn't. 3. Yes, they do. Do you drink coffee? No, we don't. 4. Yes she does. Do your parents feel all right? No, they don't. 5. Yes, you do. Do you have my telephone number? No, I don't. 6. Yes, I do. Does your friend understand Chinese? No, he doesn't. 7. Yes, they do. Does the dessert taste good? No, it doesn't. 8. Yes, it does. Do the buses leave on time? No, they don't. 9. Yes, I do. Do you wear a hat? No, I don't. 10. Yes, it does. Does the bank open at 9:00? No, it doesn't. 11. Yes, we do. Do the Wilsons own a house? No, they don't. **C:** Suggested answers: Does Flight 404 go to Boston? Yes, it does. Do Flights 404 and 612 leave in the morning? Yes, they do. Does Flight 492 leave from Gate 1? No, it doesn't. Do Flights 492 and 526 go to Japan? No, they don't.

Unit 13 A: 2. Where does 3. What do 4. When does 5. Where do 6. What do 7. Who (Whom) does 8. Where do 9. What does 10. Who (Whom) do **B:** 1. What does his wife eat? Eggs. 2. Where does your cat sleep? On the rug. 3. Who (Whom) does Mary like? Walter. 4. What does "get up" mean? Stand. 5. What does Harold watch? The news. 6. When do university classes begin? The same time. 7. When does his roommate study? After supper. **C:** Suggested answers: 2. When does the train leave for New York? At 11:00 o'clock. 3. How much does that jacket cost? It costs $100. 4. Who does that girl like? Tom Baxter. 5. Where do those men work? In the Highland Building. 6. What does the woman smell? Gas. 7. Who studies in the library in the afternoon? Tom does. 8. Where does that woman keep her jewelry? In a box in her bureau.

Unit 14 A: 1. They are getting cold. 2. It is getting cold. 3. are 4. is 5. am 6. is 7. are 8. is 9. is 10. are 11. are 12. are **B:** 2. is sleeping 3. is buying (getting) 4. is running 5. are growing 6. is making (getting/buying) 7. am working 8. are spending 9. are speaking (learning) 10. are learning 11. is getting 12. am going (running) **C:** Suggested answers: 2. The man is washing his car. 3. The boy is packing his suitcase. 4. The woman is kissing the baby. 5. He is returning the pen. 6. He is watching TV. 7. The child is crying. 8. The passengers are arriving at the airport.

Unit 15 A: 1. She isn't eating rice. 2. You aren't eating rice. 3. I'm not 4. aren't 5. isn't 6. aren't 7. isn't 8. aren't 9. aren't 10. isn't 11. isn't 12. aren't **B:** 1. We aren't drinking milk. 2. It isn't getting warm. 3. They aren't sending medicine. 4. She isn't washing the clothes. 5. I'm not writing a book. 6. She isn't moving the bed. 7. He isn't buying a suit. 8. She isn't calling the doctor. 9. He isn't helping his brother. 10. We aren't speaking German. 11. I'm not making a cake. **C:** 2. They're building a store. They aren't building a house. 3. He's reading a newspaper. He isn't reading a book. 4. She's walking. She isn't running.

Unit 16 A: 1. Are they going? Yes, they are. 2. Are we going? Yes, you/we are. 3. Are we winning? Yes, you/we are. 4. Am I winning? Yes, you are. 5. Am I winning? Yes, you are. 6. Are you losing? Yes, I am/we are. 7. Are you coming? Yes, I am/we are. 8. Is the bus coming? Yes, it is. 9. Is the bus leaving? Yes, it is. 10. Are Mr. and Mrs. Wilson leaving? Yes, they are. 11. Is your daughter leaving? Yes, she is. 12. Is your daughter calling? Yes, she is. **B:** 2. Is/correcting//he/she isn't. 3. Are/washing//they are. 4. Is/cooling//it isn't. 5. Are/having//they are. 6. Is/practicing//he isn't. 7. Am/standing//you are. 8. Are/making//they aren't. 9. Is/getting//it is. 10. Are/chewing//I'm not. 11. Are/studying//they are. 12. Is/reading//he isn't. **C:** 2. Is she skating? No, she isn't/she's not. 3. Is he eating (a sandwich)? Yes, he is. 4. Is she watching TV? Yes, she is.

Unit 17 A: 1. She's playing now. 2. She plays every morning. 3. She practices every morning. 4. She's practicing now. 5. She's swimming now. 6. She swims every week. 7. She studies every week. 8. She's studying today. 9. She's teaching today. 10. She teaches on Fridays. 11. She works on Fridays. 12. She's working this week. **B:** 1. Does he speak Spanish often? Yes, he does. But he isn't speaking Spanish now. He's speaking English. 2. Does he shop Capwell's often? Yes, he does. But he isn't shopping at Capwell's now. He's shopping at Murray's. 3. Does he drink coffee often? Yes, he does. But he isn't drinking coffee now. He's drinking tea. 4. Does he wash the car often? Yes, he does. But he isn't washing the car now. He's washing the dog. 5. Does he listen to Russian music often? Yes, he does. But he isn't listening to Russian music now. He's listening to Spanish music. 6. Does he use black ink often? Yes, he does. But he isn't using black ink now. He's using blue ink. 7. Does he watch TV often? Yes, he does. But he isn't watching TV now. He's reading a book. 8. Does he wear jeans often? Yes, he does. But he isn't wearing jeans now. He's wearing a suit. 9. Does he sit next to Darlene often? Yes, he does. But he isn't sitting next to her now. He's sitting next to Diane. 10. Does he save money often? Yes, he does. But he isn't saving money now. He's buying a motorcycle. **C:** 2. He's driving his truck to work. He paints houses. 3. She keeps recipes. She's cutting out a recipe from a magazine now. 4. He plays basketball. He's waiting on the bench now.

Unit 18 A: 1. I'm looking at that bird now. 2. I hear that bird now. 3. am listening to 4. like 5. am calling 6. want 7. am buying 8. own 9. am feeding 10. remember 11. am thinking about 12. know **B:** 2. weighs . . . is losing 3. are spending . . . equals 4. are learning . . . know 5. is trying on . . . fits 6. is speaking . . . understands 7. smell . . . smells . . . is baking 8. is looking . . . sees 9. am filling . . . holds 10. has . . . is riding **C:** 2. He's buying a toy. It costs $10.00. 3. He's looking at that new car. He wants it. 4. He's looking up "pass away." It means "die."

Unit 19 A: 1. Where's she studying? 2. When are they leaving? 3. Who is he inviting? 4. What's he cooking? 5. What's she buying? 6. Where are they swimming? 7. When are they coming? 8. What are they playing? 9. Who's she calling? **B: Suggested answers:** 1. What are you watching? An old movie. 2. What is she crying about? Her bad grades. 3. Who is she taking? Eugene. 4. Where are you going? To the post office. 5. What is she drinking? Hot chocolate. 6. What are you speaking? Italian. 7. Where are they eating? At home. 8. What are you making? A dollhouse. 9. When is he going there? On his next trip. 10. Where are you going? To the school dance. 11. What is she practicing? The violin. **C: Suggested answers:** 2. When's Mr. Long having an operation? Tomorrow. 3. What's Mrs. Forest carrying? Groceries. 4. Who's winning the basketball game? The Lions.

Unit 20 A: 3. followed /d/ 4. laughed /t/ 5. needed /ɪd/ 6. opened /d/ 7. passed /t/ 8. picked /t/ 9. played /d/ 10. pointed /ɪd/ 11. reached /t/ 12. reported /ɪd/ 13. seemed /d/ 14. wished /t/ **B:** 2. batted (A) 3. begged (A) 4. carried (C) 5. dropped (A) 6. dried (C) 7. liked (B) 8. moved (B) 9. planned (A) 10. replied (C) 11. studied (C) 12. tied (B). **C:** 2. washed 3. packed 4. kissed 5. borrowed 6. watched 7. cried 8. arrived

Unit 21 A: 1. It didn't snow. 2. He didn't pull two. 3. He didn't borrow $140. 4. She didn't pay the dentist. 5. We didn't invite the Johnsons. 6. I didn't mail Mrs. Short's letter. 7. She didn't wash the back ones. 8. We didn't visit London. 9. It didn't taste bad. 10. He didn't work on Sunday. 11. He didn't phone in the morning. 12. She/He didn't talk about love. 13. His sister didn't save two hundred dollars. 14. I didn't remember the road. 15. She didn't stop at the traffic light. 16. He didn't laugh about it. **B: Suggested answers:** 2. She didn't buy meat. She bought fish. 3. They didn't bake a cake. They baked a pie. 4. She didn't drop a glass. She dropped a vase. 5. The teacher didn't look sad. She looked happy. 6. She didn't pour milk in her glass. She poured milk on her pie.

Unit 22 A: 1. Did she work hard? 2. Did she lock the door? 3. Did she return the book? 4. Did he return the book? 5. Did he use a red pen? 6. Did he call Mr. Birch? 7. Did Andrea call Mr. Birch? 8. Did Andrea park on the street? 9. Did Andrea walk outside? 10. Did the Rowes walk outside? 11. Did the Rowes watch TV? 12. Did you watch TV? **B:** 2. No, you didn't. 3. Yes, he did. 4. No, she didn't. 5. Yes, they did. 6. No, I didn't. 7. Yes, he/she did. 8. No, it didn't. 9. Yes, it did. 10. No, she didn't. 11. Yes, he did. 12. No, she didn't. **C:** 2. Yes, she did. Did she break her tennis racket? 3. Yes, he did. Did he leave any cookies? 4. No, it didn't. Did it cost 40 cents? 5. No, they didn't. Did they wear light clothes?

Unit 23 A: 1. Did you sell your car? No, but I sold my bike. 2. Did you hear Billie? No, but I heard Susie. 3. Did you hurt your leg? No, but I hurt my foot. 4. Did you make the table? No, but I made the desk. 5. Did you shut the door? No, but I shut the window. 6. Did you hit your head? No, but I hit my arm. 7. Did you tell John? No, but I told Henry. 8. Did you do the housework? No, but I did the errands. **B:** 1. I heard a loud noise. 2. He shut the upstairs window. 3. She had a big glass of orange juice. 4. He sold his old TV. 5. He told Annabelle. 6. He did his math homework. 7. It cost fifty thousand dollars. 8. It hit a small tree. 9. She said yes. 10. He did the dinner dishes. 11. He put his lamp there. 12. It cost two hundred dollars. 13. She shut her book. **C: Suggested answers:** 2. That boy made a kite. 3. She put out that candle. 4. He sold his motorcycle.

Unit 24 A: 2. slept 3. sent (bought, brought) 4. lost 5. thought 6. felt 7. left 8. caught 9. built 10. brought 11. taught 12. bought 13. lent 14. spent 15. meant **B:** 1. Did you lose your ring? No, I didn't lose my ring. I lost my watch. 2. Did you leave the office at 6:00? No, I didn't leave at 6:00. I left at 5:00. 3. Did you build a model car? No, I didn't build a model car. I built a model airplane. 4. Did you spend $50? No, I didn't spend $50. I spent $30. 5. Did you teach Spanish? No, I didn't teach Spanish. I taught French. 6. Did you bring a salad? No, I didn't bring a salad. I brought a dessert. 7. Did you catch the 7:00 bus? No, I didn't catch the 7:00 bus. I caught the 8:00 bus. 8. Did you go to a movie yesterday afternoon? No, I didn't go to a movie yesterday afternoon. I went home. **C:** 2. meant/said 3. bought//spent 4. left/caught

Unit 25 A: 1. Did Gary take a bus? No, he took a taxi. 2. Did Gary speak Italian? No, he spoke French. 3. Did Gary read a newspaper? No, he read a magazine. 4. Did Gary win $500? No, he won $100. 5. Did Gary meet Tom? No, he met his brother. 6. Did Gary drink coffee? No, he drank tea. 7. Did Gary find money? No, he found a wallet. 8. Did Gary sing in German? No, he sang in Russian. 9. Did Gary get a new car? No, he got an old car (one). **B: Suggested answers:** 1. He got home late. 2. His roommate met him (at the door). 3. His roommate gave him some. 4. He ate a sandwich. 5. He wore red pajamas. 6. He went to the movies. 7. No, he read two pages of a book. 8. The doorbell woke him up. It was 10:00 p.m. 9. The telephone woke him up at 2:00 a.m. 12. The alarm clock woke John up at 6:00 a.m. 13. No, he didn't go back to sleep. He got up. 14. No, I don't think he felt fine.

Unit 26 A: 2. drew 3. grew 4. understood 5. lay (sat) 6. ran 7. stood 8. flew 9. knew 10. fell 11. rode 12. saw 13. held **B: Suggested answers:** 1. No, she sat. No, he stood. 2. She flew. She drove. 3. He broke his leg. He fell (from some rocks). 4. No, they ran home. **C:** 1. I saw it two nights ago. 2. He came two days ago. 3. He fell two weeks ago. 4. She found out two months ago. 5. He wrote it two days ago. 6. I drove it a few days ago. 7. She broke it two days ago. 8. He flew many years ago.

Unit 27 A: 1. She thought about food. 2. She wanted to protect the flowers. 3. She missed her parents. 4. He said I'm sorry. 5. She taught Greek. 6. She stayed in a hotel. 7. He played the piano. 8. He grew apples. 9. She drove a tractor. 10. He wanted a dictionary. 11. It hit a tree. 12. She changed the sheets. 13. She sold her watch. 14. He watched a soccer game. 15. He sat on the grass. 16. She gave her her sandwich. 17. He brought a cake. 18. He cut his face. 19. She moved the sofa. 20. He ate lunch. 21. He took some rings. **B:** Suggested answers: 1. No, he met him at Ames Airport. 2. He had one on Tuesday, July 10. 3. He had lunch with Jim Weaver. 4. He went to Chicago. 5. He flew. 6. He left at 1:00 p.m. on Thursday. 7. He took Jane.

Unit 28 A: 1. Where did you teach? 2. When did it return? 3. What did he/she do? 4. When did it end? 5. Where did he lose it? 6. Who did she bring? 7. What did she hear? 8. What did he/she take? 9. Who did she see? **B:** Suggested answers: 1. Where did he teach? At St. Louis University. 2. Where did you eat? At the China Garden Restaurant. 3. What did you drink? Hot chocolate. 4. Where did they meet? On a plane. 5. What did you study? Foreign languages. 6. Where did it sail from? (From) Dublin. 7. What did she wear? Jeans. 8. Who did she tell? Sherri. 9. When did they start? In October. 10. Who did he take? Harriet. 11. What did you say? Hope. **C:** Suggested answers: 2. Where did he take them to dinner? He took them to Sam's. 3. Who did the girls bring to the swimming pool? They brought a little boy. 4. When did the plane land? It landed at 10:45. 5. Who answered the phone? The young woman answered it. 6. When did they eat breakfast? They ate at 7:30.

Unit 29 A: 1. Carlos was learning English. 2. Carlos was speaking English. 3. The children were speaking. . . . 4. The children were practicing. . . . 5. I was practicing. . . . 6. I was using. . . . 7. They were using. . . . 8. They were reading. . . . 9. They were writing. . . . 10. You were writing. . . . 11. Miss Osawa was writing. . . . 12. Miss Osawa was teaching. . . . **B:** 1. The tenants weren't wasting gas. They were wasting electricity. 2. Julia wasn't reading a magazine. She was reading a book. 3. Mr. Harrison wasn't selling washing machines. He was selling office machines. 4. My father wasn't looking at the newspaper. He was taking a nap. 5. The Joneses weren't living in a house. They were living in an apartment. 6. We weren't borrowing money. We were lending it. 7. Penny wasn't writing letters. She was making phone calls. 8. You weren't managing the company. You were working for it. 9. I wasn't buying the house. I was renting it. 10. Fred wasn't paying cash. He was using a credit card. 11. Mr. Michaels wasn't saving any money. He was spending it all. **C:** Suggested answers: 1. He was riding a bicycle. 2. No, he wasn't leaving the office. He was talking on the phone. He was working on a/his car. 3. No, she wasn't studying. She was practicing the piano. 4. She was shopping. No, she wasn't taking a nap. She was cooking. She was cooking chicken.

Unit 30 A: 1. Were they following the cat? 2. Were you following the cat? 3. Were you touching. . . . 4. Was he touching. . . . 5. Was he hurting. . . . 6. Was I hurting. . . . 7. Were both of you hurting. . . . 8. Were the dogs hurting . . . . 9. Were the dogs watching. . . . 10. Was your aunt watching. . . . 11. Was your aunt calling. . . . 12. Were you and Helen calling. . . . **B:** 2. Was he sitting on the ground? No, he wasn't. 3. Was John buying stamps? Yes, he was. 4. Were we going to Chicago then? No, we weren't. 5. Was Mr. Florence cashing a check? Yes, he was. 6. Were you depositing money? No, I wasn't/we weren't. 7. Were they speaking Italian? Yes, they were. 8. Were your parents working at the same company? No, they weren't. 9. Was the woman locking the door? Yes, she was. 10. Was Harry starting a restaurant? No, he wasn't. 11. Was the snow covering the leaves in the road? Yes, it was. 12. Were the students waiting on the wrong corner? No, they weren't. **C:** 2. Was Dr. Ford working last Tuesday afternoon? Yes, he was. He was performing an operation. Was Dr. Nelson working last Tuesday afternoon? No, he wasn't. He was playing golf. 3. Was Joyce writing at 10:00 last night? Yes, she was. She was writing letters. Was Ted writing at 10:00 last night? No, he wasn't. He was sleeping.

Unit 31 A: 2. met//was looking 3. heard//was sewing 4. ran//were burning 5. bought//was wearing 6. made//hurt 7. heard//was playing 8. got//was ringing 9. was//running; fell//hurt 10. broke//was chewing **B:** 1. They were waiting in Philadelphia at 4:30 p.m. 2. They were sleeping at midnight 3. arrived 4. spent 5. got 6. crossed 7. were going 8. were 9. crossed 10. saw 11. got

Unit 32 A: 1. We're going to catch fish. 2. He's going to catch fish. 3. He's going to eat fish. 4. I'm going to eat fish. 5. I'm going to order fish. 6. They're going to order fish. 7. They're going to sell fish. 8. The company's going to sell fish. 9. The company's going to pack fish. 10. You're going to pack fish. 11. You're going to cook fish. 12. You're going to serve fish. **B:** 1. The children aren't going to ski. They're going to skate. 2. We aren't going to eat potatoes. We're going to eat rice. 3. Laura isn't going to write novels. She's going to write poems. 4. Mrs. Wright isn't going to change the curtains. She's going to change the rug. 5. Harry isn't going to pay the gas bill. He's going to pay the electric bill. 6. Jenny isn't going to walk to work. She's going to take the bus. 7. I'm not going to waste time. I'm going to finish this work. 8. The company isn't going to write a letter. They're going to phone them. 9. The bakers aren't going to use old eggs. They're going to get fresh ones. 10. Dolly isn't going to sign her full name. She's going to use her initials. 11. Lisa isn't going to leave the car on the street. She's going to park in the driveway. **C:** Suggested answers: 1. John isn't going to walk. He's going to ride a bike. 2. Mary isn't going to play cards. She's going to see a movie. Alice isn't going to swim. She's going to go to the dentist. 3. The Martins aren't going to go to Maine. They're going to visit New York City. The Adamses aren't going to go to the seashore. They're going to go to the mountains.

Unit 33 A: 1. Is she going to paint the house? 2. Are they going to paint the house? 3. Are they going to fix up the house? 4. Are they going to fix up the car? 5. Are they going to sell the car? 6. Is Alice going to sell the car? 7. Is Bill going to sell the car? 8. Is Bill going to return the car? 9. Is Bill going to return the library books? 10. Are they going to return the library books? 11. Are they going to return the money? 12. Is the insurance company going to return the money? **B:** 1. Is he going to get well? No, he isn't. 2. Is the tea going to cool off? Yes, it is. 3. Is water going to get . . . it isn't. 4. Is Judith going to get . . . she is. 5. Is it going to rain . . . it isn't. 6. Is coal going to go . . . it is. 7. Are you going to use . . . I am. 8. Are the children going to read . . . they aren't. 9. Are you going to wear . . . I am. 10. Is Mr. Longworth going to buy . . . he isn't. 11. Are we going to stop . . . we are. **C:** Suggested answers: Is the tennis match going to be on Thursday, March 2? No, it isn't. They aren't going to have that tennis match. Are the Eagles and Jays going to play basketball on Friday, March 3? Yes, they are. The game's going to begin at 7 p.m. Is the swimming meet going to be on Saturday, March 4? Yes, it is. It's going to begin at 2:30 p.m.

Unit 34 A: 1. She will be good. 2. She will look good. 3. You will look good. 4. Stan and he will look good. 5. Stan and he will feel good. 6. I will feel good. 7. It will feel good. 8. It will smell good. 9. It will sound good. 10. The car will sound good. 11. Her English will sound good. 12. Your voice will sound good. **B:** 1. I won't take Spanish. I'll take German. 2. She won't wear a skirt. She'll wear jeans. 3. She won't talk . . . She'll talk. . . . 4. The company won't raise . . . They'll make. . . . 5. They won't mail . . . They'll deliver. . . . 6. Mr. Steger won't forget . . . He'll call . . . . 7. The wedding won't be . . . It'll cost. . . . 8. Mrs. Gordon won't call . . . She'll call. . . . 9. These watches won't break . . . They'll give. . . . 10. The weather won't improve. It'll be. . . . 11. Miss Baker won't buy . . . She'll drive . . . . **C:** Suggested answers: 2. This tour won't go to Madrid. It'll go to Paris. 3. She won't give the motorcycle a ticket. She'll give the car a ticket. 4. The repairs won't cost $300. They'll cost $250.

Unit 35 A: 1. Will they pack lunch? 2. Will he pack lunch? 3. Will you pack 4. Will you carry 5. Will Mr. Williams carry 6. Will the children carry 7. Will the children buy 8. Will your boss buy 9. Will your boss make 10. Will we make 11. Will we need 12. Will I need **B:** 1. Will she eat the peaches? Yes, she will. 2. Will the scissors cut this box? No, it won't. 2. Will Donald sit . . . he will. 4. Will your uncle bring . . . he won't. 5. Will the eggs be . . . they will. 6. Will the flag stay . . . it won't. 7. Will Patty answer . . . she will. 8. Will her cousin be . . . it won't. 9. Will those books cost . . . it will. 10. Will these tires go . . . they won't. **C:** Suggested answers: 1. Will Flight 291 arrive at 5:20? No, it won't. Will the Boston plane come in this afternoon? No, it won't. Will Flight 414 land today? No, it won't. 2. Will the woman jump out of the window? No, she won't. Will the firemen put water on the fire? Yes, they will. Will they put out the fire? Yes, they will. Will they save the woman and baby? Yes, they will.

Unit 36 A: 1. Where will we meet? At the restaurant on 16th Street. 2. Who will we invite to the party? Jim, Bill, Ted, and Alice. 3. What will she tell Jim? The truth. 4. When will the wedding take place? On June 6. 5. Where will the wedding be? At St. Michael's Church. 6. When will they pay the bill. (On) the first of next month. 7. Where will the meeting be held? In Room 607. 8. Who will meet us at the airport? The tour director. 9. What will I give Mary for her birthday? A watch. **B:** Suggested answers: Who is Mrs. Jones going to pick up at the bus station on Monday afternoon? She's going to pick up Ted. What's she going to do at 5:30 on Tuesday? She's going to pick up Ted at the office. Where is Mrs. Jones going to have lunch with Florence on Monday? She's going to have lunch at the El Patio Restaurant. Where is she going to buy toothpaste? She's going to buy it at the drugstore. What are Helen and Edith going to do on Wednesday morning. They're going to go shopping.

Unit 37 A: Suggested answers: When do the Yankees and Bears play? They play on June 14. When do the White Sox play the Penguins? They play them on Thursday, June 4th. When are the Cardinals playing the Giants? They're playing them on Friday the 13th. When are the Lions and Bears playing baseball? They're playing on June 3. **B:** 2. Is Georgie going to be an engineer? No, he's going to be a (h) 3. Will your daughter get a job in the fall? No, she'll (f) 4. Are you taking the 9:00 flight tomorrow? No, I'm taking (i) 5. Are you and your wife going to buy a house this year? No, we're going to (a) 6. Will the wedding be cheap? No, it'll be (b) 7. Will you be in Europe next year at this time? No, we'll (g) 8. Are you going to stay home tonight? No, I'm going to (d) 9. Is Annie going to save her allowance? No, she's going to (e) 10. Will the meeting be interesting? No, it'll be (j)

Unit 38 A: 1. He can skate. He can't ski. 2. She can play cards. She can't play chess. 3. He can play . . . He can't play . . . . 4. I can fix . . . I can't fix. . . . 5. You can see . . . You can't see. . . . 6. We can go . . . We can't go. . . . 7. They can change . . . They can't change. . . . 8. Paul can speak . . . He can't speak. . . . 9. Maria can shut . . . She can't lock. . . . 10. Tom can spend . . . He can't save . . . . 11. Miss Neuman can type . . . She can't take. . . . **B:** 1. Can you hear the phone? Yes, I can. 2. Can he lift that chair? No, he can't. 3. Can she run . . . she can. 4. Can they come . . . they can't. 5. Can they sell . . . they can. 6. Can you read . . . I can't. 7. Can she make . . . she can't. 8. Can Mr. Schlieper . . . he can't. 9. Can you buy . . . you can. 10. Can you understand . . . I can't. 11. Can horses swim? . . . they can. **C:** Suggested answers: 2. Can the young man swim well? No, he can't. 3. Can Ted eat food? No, he can't.

Unit 39 A: 1. I have to be home. 2. You have to be home. 3. You want to be home. 4. You want to stay home. 5. We want to stay home. 6. We don't want to stay home. 7. She doesn't want to stay home. 8. They don't want to stay home. 9. I don't want to stay home. 10. I don't have to stay home. 11. John doesn't have to stay home. 12. John doesn't have to leave home. **B:** 1. Do you have to stay in bed? Yes, I do. 2. Do you want to play basketball? No, I don't. 3. Do you have to pay . . . I don't. 4. Do you want to take . . . I do. 5. Do you have to paint . . . I do. 6. Do you want to see . . . I don't. 7. Do you have to make . . . I do. 8. Do you want to sell . . . I do. 9. Do you have to get . . . I do. 10. Do you want to march . . . I don't. 11. Do you have to go . . . I don't. **C:** Suggested answers: 2. Does he want to play baseball? Yes, but he has to practice the piano. 3. Does she want to eat that pie? Yes, but she has to stay away from rich food. 4. Do they want to buy the expensive TV? Yes, but they have to buy the cheap one.

Unit 40 A: 2. stops, stopping, stopped 3. read, reading, read 4. buy, buys, bought 5. begin, begins, beginning 6. sends, sending, sent 7. win, winning, won 8. have, has, had 9. drive, drives, driving **B:** 2. made 3. barking 4. visit 5. trying 6. pay **C:** 2. eating 3. owns 4. watched 5. see 6. walked 7. cost/costs 8. arriving

Unit 41 A: 1. Debbie wasn't. She wasn't in the garage either. 2. Eric can't. He can't play the piano either. 3. Flo won't. She won't graduate in January either. 4. Gary isn't. He isn't taking German either. 5. Her husband doesn't. He doesn't write many postcards either. 6. The policeman didn't. He didn't see the fight either. 7. His friend isn't. He/She isn't a good writer either. 8. Mr. Gale wasn't. He wasn't on time for Ted's speech either. 9. Heather isn't. She isn't going to be here either. 10. Jim wasn't. He wasn't studying at the library either. 11. Ann and Alice don't. They don't drive trucks either. 12. Bob and Bill didn't. They didn't swim on Sunday either. 13. Don and Dave weren't. They weren't in my math class either. 14. Mary and Monica aren't. They aren't studying math either. 15. The Eagles don't. They don't have a good coach either. **B:** Suggested answers: 2. The traffic isn't moving (can't) move. 3. The policeman doesn't like this job. 4. That businessman won't get in the taxi. 5. Burgerworld isn't open. 6. The window washer isn't working.

Unit 42 A: 2. Did they play hockey? No, they didn't. Did they slalom? Yes, they did. 3. Does he slalom? No, he doesn't. Does he ski jump? Yes, he does. 4. Is she skiing? No, she isn't. Is she speed skating? Yes, she is. 5. Were they speed skating? No, they weren't. Were they figure skating? Yes, they were. 6. Will they bobsled? No, they won't. Will they play hockey? Yes, they will. **B:** Suggested answers: Is Nick going to see the final hockey game? Yes, he is. Will Laura and Nick beat Mt. Oleg on Wednesday? No, they won't. Did Laura see the bobsled races? No, she didn't. Was Nick at the women's speed skating on Monday? No, he wasn't. Are Laura and Nick watching the slalom now? Yes, they are.

Unit 43 A: 2. chicken,bird 3. bread,food 4. water,liquid 5. building,school 6. coin,quarter 7. book,dictionary 8. street,Main Street 9. Mary,sister 10. Friday,birthday 11. neighbor,teacher 12. shirt,cotton. **B:** 2. cap,table 3. tea, ground 4. man,tree 5. stick,hand 6. child,car **C:** 1. mailman/letter/table 2. lady/money/counter 3. cashier/change/counter 4. student/picture/wall 5. man/toothpaste/toothbrush 6. boy/tail/kite 7. girl/dress/doll 8. waiter/lemon/fish 9. child/jelly/bread 10. waiter/food/table

Unit 44 A: /z/: 2. bowls 4. days 6. ears 7. guns 9. names 13. roads 15. stoves 17. things 18. tubs; /s/: 1. books 3. moths 8. hats 14. safes 16. tapes; /ɪz/: 5. dishes 10. noses 11. pages 12. pieces 19. watches **B:** 2. girls/z/,films/z/ 3. nurses /ɪz/,hands/z/ 4. plants/s/,months/s/ 5. tests/s/,parts/s/ 6. lamps/s/,bulbs/z/ 7. books/s/,pages/ɪz/ 8. farms/z/,barns/z/ 9. fields/z/, fences/ɪz/ 10. changes/ɪz/, words/z/ 11. parks/s/,churches/ɪz/ 12. banks/s/,gifts/s/ **C:** Suggested answers: 2. The puppies have collars. 3. The pencils have erasers. 4. The garages have cars inside.

Unit 45 A: 2. three men 3. five fish 4. two mice 5. six knives 6. two halves 7. four wolves 8. three loaves **B:** 2. shelves 3. women 4. children 5. thieves 6. lives 7. geese,sheep 8. Deer,leaves 9. wives 10. mouths **C:** 1. Do you see a mouse? No, I see two mice. 2. fish,fish 3. tooth, teeth 4. child,children 5. woman, women 6. calf,calves 7. wolf,wolves 8. foot,feet 9. path,paths

Unit 46 A: 1. eggs 2. egg 3. egg 4. eggs 5. egg 6. egg (or eggs) 7. egg (or eggs) 8. eggs 9. egg (or eggs) 10. eggs 11. egg 12. eggs (or egg) 13. eggs 14. egg 15. egg (or eggs) 16. eggs (or egg) 17. egg (or eggs) 18. eggs 19. egg 20. eggs 21. egg (or eggs) **B:** 2. tests,teacher 3. letters,word 4. sleeves,dress 5. box, nuts 6. roof,windows 7. coats,closet 8. keys,hotel 9. hour,minutes 10. chicken,vegetables 11. pictures,door 12. machine,cigarettes **C:** 1. What has seven days? A week. 2. What has three sides? A triangle. 3. What has two wings? A bird. 4. What has two wheels? A bicycle. 5. What has four legs? A bed. 6. What has six pockets? A pool table.

Unit 47 A: 2. cigarettes d,f 3. clothing d 4. milk b,d 5. parties e 6. snow a,e 7. candy d,f,h 8. big words c,e **B:** 1. Did Mike want some matches? No, he wanted some wood. 2. some bags, some string 3. some paper, some pencils 4. some gas, some tires 5. some combs, some toothpaste 6. some information, some money 7. some books, some music 8. some film, some stamps 9. some water, some water glasses 10. some corn, some tomatoes 11. some rocks, some sand **C:** 2. an apple 3. a drop of coffee 4. a box of cereal 5. a quarter 6. a piece of cake

Unit 48 A: 2. 's/s/ 3. 's/ɪz/ 4. 's/ɪz/ 5. 's/z/ 6. 's/z/ 7. 's/s/ 8. 's/ɪz/ 9. 's/z/ 10. 's /s/ 11. 's /z/ 12. 's /s/ 13. 's /z/ 14. 's /ɪz/ **B:** 1. people's money 2. buses' wheels 3. sheep's wool 4. countries' flags 5. waitresses' uniforms 6. workers' pay 7. children's beds 8. the parks' trees 9. the Chatmans' bank account 10. whales' teeth 11. speakers' microphones **C:** 2. nurse's 3. car's 4. cats' 5. players' 6. uncle's

Unit 49 A: 2. pilot,pilot's,pilots,pilots' 3. wife,wife's,wives,wives' 4. mouse, mouse's,mice,mice's 5. boss,boss's, bosses, bosses' 6. baby,baby's,babies, babies' **B:** 1. teacher's 2. sister's 3. workers' 4. flowers 5. clowns 6. shoes 7. circus's 8. teacher 9. children 10. woman's 11. phone 12. nurse's **C:** 2. families 3. women's 4. Herb's 5. teachers' 6. wives 7. taxis 8. boss's 9. Sundays 10. tooth 11. farmers 12. cow's

Unit 50 A: 1. That looks like a bottle. 2. a 3. a 4. an (8, 14, and 21 are *an*; the rest are *a*.) **B:** 1. We had a hard test today. 2. an active child 3. a young artist 4. an honest student 5. an unhappy message 6. a strange accident 7. an old hat 8. a quick meeting 9. an early train 10. an interesting speech 11. a useful trip 12. a hot oven **C:** 2. a painter and a teacher 3. an elephant and a mouse 4. an envelope and a stamp 5. an apple and a banana 6. a ride in an airplane

Unit 51 A: 2. the radio 3. the library 4. the left 5. The sun 6. the driver 7. the living room 8. the receptionist **B:** 2. the same 3. the fourth (or a warm) 4. the only 5. The worst 6. the next 7. the wrong 8. The last **C:** Suggested answers: 2. Yes, the bill was (for) $86.00. 3. Yes, the call is from Janice. 4. Yes, the meeting will be (held) in Room 206. 5. Yes, the telephone is (over) there.

Unit 52 A: Suggested answers: 1. I borrowed a book. The cover was dirty. 2. I visited a farm. The animals were healthy. 3. I looked at a house. The kitchen was too small. 4. I used a pen. The ink was too light. 5. She carried a handbag. The strap was very long. 6. He took an exam. The room was very quiet. 7. I bought a clock. The alarm was very loud. 8. I have a bicycle. The seat is too high. 9. I read an article. The subject was interesting. **B:** 2. the 3. the,the 4. an 5. the 6. a 7. the 8. the,the 9. the,a 10. the,a 11. a,the,the 12. The, a,the **C:** 2. I'll take an apple. I don't want the orange. 3. I'll use a cup. I don't want the glass. 4. I'll sit in a chair. I won't sit on the sofa.

Unit 53 A: 1. I'll write the parent's name and the child's. 2. I'll write the boss's name and the secretary's. 3. I'll write the teacher's name and the student's. 4. I'll write the lawyer's name and the judge's. 5. I'll write the police officer's name and the thief's. 6. I'll write the company's name and the president's. 7. I'll write the hunter's name and the dog's. 8. I'll write the town's name and the street's. 9. I'll write the baby's name and the mother's. **B:** 1. Is Dawn Max and Eve's daughter? No, she's Bob and Hope's. 2. Is Eve Bob's wife? No, she's Max's. 3. Is Doug Hope's husband? No, he's Rose's. 4. Is Dick Ruth's brother? No, he's Dawn's. 5. Is Ray Bob and Hope's son? No, He's Max and Eve's. 6. Is Max Dick's father? No, he's Rose's, Ray's and Ruth's. 7. Is Eve Dawn's mother? No, she's Rose's, Ray's and Ruth's. **C:** 1. No, it's Mike's. 2. No, they're Mary's. 3. No, they're my son's slippers. 4. No, it was the typist's. 5. No, they're my wife's dresses. 6. No, he's the manager's brother.

Unit 54 A: 1. No, he has a big bank account. 2. No, he has a good typewriter. 3. No, they make good jeans. 4. No, they served hot coffee. 5. No, she used sharp scissors. 6. No, she picked the ripe cucumbers. 7. No, he's wearing a blue sweater. 8. No, she's eating a sour peach. 9. No, it was a windy night. 10. No, they're washing the dirty truck. 11. No, they sold the old plane. **B:** 1. No, I have a small one. 2. No, I took the right one. 3. No, he took the late one. 4. No, it was a very hard one. 5. No, she uses a cheap one. 6. No, she bought red ones. 7. No, we had a rainy one. 8. No, they wore short ones. 9. No, I prefer German ones. 10. No, she took the dirty ones. 11. No, it's on a noisy one. **C:** Suggested answers: 2. A terrible one. 3. The large ones. 4. The big one.

Unit 55 A: 2. second/next 3. third 4. fourth 5. fifth/next 6. sixth 7. seventh/last 8. first 9. second 10. third 11. sixth 12. fourth 13. fifth 14. last/seventh **B:** 1. It's the ninth (month). 2. I celebrate my birthday. 3. It's the hundred and second (floor). 4. It's due on May twenty-fifth. 5. He was the sixteenth (president). 6. It finished in eighth (place). 7. We're studying the fifty-fifth (unit).

Unit 56 A: 2. these, this 3. this, these 4. these, this 5. this, these 6. This, these 8. that, those 9. those, that 10. that, those 11. that, those 12. those, that **B:** 1. Is this the dining room? No, that's the dining room. 2. Are these gold rings? No, those are gold rings. 3. Is this . . . 4. Is this 5. Are these 6. Is this 7. Are these 8. Is this 9. Are these **C:** 2. Those come from California. 3. This one makes boxes. 4. That one goes to Martinez. 5. C. M. Jourdan wrote those.

Unit 57 A: Suggested answers: 1. The other city is far away. 2. The other women have long hair. 3. The other streets are quiet. 4. The other child ate a sandwich. 5. The other days weren't sunny. 6. The other movie wasn't American. 7. The other dessert is expensive. 8. She didn't do well in the other subjects. 9. We learned (a) little from the other teacher. 10. I don't have $6,000 in the other bank. **B:** 2. other instruments 3. other restaurants 4. other trips 5. another TV set 6. another doctor 7. Other students 8. another exam **C:** 2. They paid the gas. They didn't pay the other bills. 3. I visited Mary. I'll visit another friend soon. 4. They don't grow corn. They grow other vegetables.

Unit 58 A: 1. One was long. The other one was not long. 2. One is there. The others are in Room 210. 3. One is plastic. The others are glass. 4. One is a bank. The other one is a library. 5. One was a doctor. The others were engineers. 6. One arrives in the morning. The other one arrives in the afternoon. 7. Five were new. The other one was very old. 8. Five are taking English. The other one is taking French. 9. Three are having sales. The others are not having sales. 10. Twelve live there. The other one lives in Emeryville. **B:** 2. others 3. others 4. another one 5. another one 6. another one 7. others 8. others **C:** 2. One policeman is fat. The other is thin. 3. One suitcase is Bob's. Another is Paul's. The others are Robbie's. 4. Four windows are open. The others are closed. 5. One squirrel is climbing. Another is drinking. The other is getting nuts. 6. One newspaper is from Britain. Another is from Argentina. The others are from Mexico.

Unit 59 A: you, I, We, you, We, I **B:** 2. e. She 3. a. They 4. b. He 5. f. It 6. d. They **C:** Suggested answers: 2. She's writing a letter. 3. It fell on a lamp. 4. I'm at the store. 5. Yes, they are on their way home. 6. He lifts weights.

Unit 60 A: 1. Are you and Robert coming? Yes, Tom just called us. 2. Is Martha coming? Yes, . . . her. 3. them 4. him 5. her 6. her 7. them 8. him/her 9. me 10. her 11. you 12. us **B:** 2. it 3. them 4. him 5. them 6. us 7. me 8. her 9. him 10. it/him/her 11. you 12. us 13. her 14. it 15. them **C:** Suggested answers: 1. Yes, I like her. 2. Yes, I know him. (or) No, I don't know him. 3. I put them by the bed. 4. I put it on the wall.

Unit 61 A: 1. I keep my car there. 2. She keeps her money there. 3. keep their 4. keep our 5. keep their 6. keeps his 7. keeps her 8. keep their 9. keep your 10. keep their 11. keeps its **B:** 2. e. Our 3. a. their 4. d. its 5. g. your 6. c. her 7. b. His 8. h. your **C:** 2. She's warming her hands. He's standing by/near the fire. 3. It's missing its hands. It's missing its cover. 4. She forgot her coat. He'll give her his coat.

Unit 62 A: 1. I didn't buy the picture. You did. Then it's mine. 2. You didn't buy the book. The employees did. Then it's theirs. 3. his 4. his 5. hers

6. ours 7. theirs 8. yours 9. his/hers 10. ours **B:** 2. ours 3. his 4. ours 5. hers 6. Mine 7. Theirs 8. Ours 9. mine 10. Hers 11. his 12. his **C:** 2. mine 3. theirs 4. Yours, ours

Unit 63 A: 1. We almost burned ourselves. 2. They almost burned themselves. 3. yourself/yourselves 4. myself 5. themselves 6. yourselves 7. herself 8. herself 9. himself 10. ourselves 11. itself/himself/herself 12. themselves **B:** 2. themselves 3. themselves 4. itself 5. ourselves 6. himself 7. himself 8. herself 9. herself 10. myself 11. themselves 12. myself 13. himself 14. yourself/yourselves 15. itself **C:** Suggested answers: 2. He sees himself in the mirror. 3. She surprised herself. 4. She bought herself a swimsuit.

Unit 64 A: 2. she likes him 3. and I remember them 4. and he believed me 5. and we're helping her 6. and I need you 7. and you're touching it 8. and they wanted us **B:** 2. theirs 3. He, himself 4. me 5. his 6. its/his/her 7. They 8. her 9. her 10. She, herself 11. hers. 12. it 13. his, He, himself 14. mine 15. us 16. yourselves **C:** I, my, I, yours, my, your, mine, I, yourself

Unit 65 A: 1. We need some cotton, but we don't need any wool. 2. We need some apples, but we don't need any lemons. 3. some soap//any toothpaste 4. some envelopes//any stamps 5. some potatoes// any rice 6. some gas// any oil 7. some cups//any glasses 8. some tea//any coffee 9. some blue pens//any red pens 10. some clerks// any nurses 11. some water//any food **B:** 1. Do you want some/any pie? No, thanks. I don't want any. 2. Do you want some/any salad? Yes. please. I'd like some. 3. some bread, any 4. any peaches, some 5. any beans, any 6. any butter, some 7. some oranges, some 8. any salt, any 9. any water, any 10. some nuts, some 11. any fish, some 12. any cherries, any **C:** Suggested answers: 2. any//Yes, some got on the floor. 3. any//No, he didn't leave any. 4. any//Yes, she typed some. 5. any// No, she didn't eat any. 6. any//Yes, some talked to her.

Unit 66 A: 1. She bought some perfume. 2. She bought a jacket. 3. some 4. some 5. an 6. some 7. a 8. some 9. an 10. some 11. a 12. some **B:** 2. some 3. any 4. an 5. A 6. Some 7. Some 8. any 9. a, one 10. some, some 11. some, any 12. an, some 13. some, any 14. a, one 15. some, any 16. any, some **C:** 2. She bought some fish, but she didn't buy any chicken. 3. He had some dimes, but he didn't have any quarters. 4. He ordered some paper, but he didn't order any tape. 5. They planted some vegetables, but they didn't plant any flowers. 6. He put on some salt, but he didn't put on any pepper.

Unit 67 A: 1. I don't have much money. 2. I don't have many pennies. 3. many 4. much 5. many 6. much 7. much 8. many 9. many 10. much 11. many 12. much **B:** 1. Do you read books? Yes, but not many. 2. Do you see movies? Yes, but not many. 3. much 4. much 5. much 6. much 7. many 8. many 9. much 10. many 11. many 12. much **C:** 2. She didn't bake many cookies. 3. They aren't growing many tomatoes. 4. He doesn't own many shoes. 5. She didn't wash many clothes. 6. He isn't using much paint.

Unit 68 A: 1. He bought a lot of milk. 2. He didn't buy much fruit. 3. He bought a lot of corn. 4. He didn't buy many cookies. 5. He bought a lot of sugar. 6. He didn't buy many hot dogs. 7. He didn't buy much toothpaste. 8. He bought a lot of light bulbs. 9. He didn't buy many paper napkins. 10. He didn't buy much fruit. **B:** 2. a lot of/many 3. much 4. many 5. a lot of 6. a lot of 7. much/a lot of 8. many/a lot of 9. many/a lot of 10. a lot 11. much/a lot 12. many/a lot 13. Many/A lot 14. many/a lot 15. many/a lot

Unit 69 A: 1. She needs a little butter. 2. She needs a few eggs. 3. a little 4. a few 5. a little 6. a few 7. a little 8. a few 9. a little 10. a little 11. a little 12. a few. **B:** 1. A few did. 2. A little did. 3. A few do. 4. A little does. 5. A few did. 6. A few do. 7. A few did. 8. A few are. 9. A little is. 10. A few were. 11. A little was. 12. A few were. **C:** Suggested answers: 2. What is he ordering? He's ordering a little tape/ typing paper. 3. What did he use? He used a few tools. 4. What will she take on the trip? She'll take a few books.

Unit 70 A: 2. little 3. Few 4. few 5. little 6. little 7. Few 8. Few 9. Few 10. Few 11. little 12. Few **B:** 1. We're getting few vegetables. 2. We're getting little rain. 3. He forgets few names. 4. That school has few Latin American students. 5. That teacher gives no tests. 6. Little water spilled on the floor. 7. He has no money. 8. Little cold air got into the room. **C:** 2. coffee, none 3. people, few 4. paper, little 5. medicine, none 6. cookies, none

Unit 71 A: 1. She borrowed some of your keys. 2. She borrowed some of these keys. 3. three of these 4. a few of these 5. a few of my 6. a few of those 7. many of those 8. many of the 9. few of the 10. a lot of the 11. a couple of the 12. none of the **B:** Suggested answers: 2. some of the toys 3. one of the pencils 4. some of that ice cream 5. many of the cookies 6. one of her slippers 7. two of the windows **C:** 2. none of 3. one of 4. any/some of 5. a few of 6. few of 7. much of 8. one of 9. a little of 10. much of 11. A little of 12. One of

Unit 72 A: 2. Both 3. All 4. each 5. Every 6. all 7. all 8. Every . . . All 9. All, Every 10. each, Both **B:** Suggested answers: 1. Did she break both of them? Yes, she did. 2. Did he read all of them? Yes, he did. 3. Did he/she pass both of them? Yes, he/she did. 4. Does he like both of them? Yes, he does. 5. Did you grow all of them? Yes, we did. 6. Did he give a souvenir to each of them? Yes, he did. 7. Did he/she mark every one of them? Yes, he/she did. 8. Do each of them run well? Yes, they do. 9. Did every one of them die? Yes, they did. **C:** 2. all 3. Each 4. All (of) 5. both 6. each 7. all of 8. Each

Unit 73 A: 1. Do they spend a quarter of their money on taxes and insurance? No, (only) an eighth of it. 2. Do they spend half of their money on utilities and repairs? No, (only) a sixteenth of it. 3. Do they spend a quarter of their money on food? No, (only) an eighth of it. 4. Do they spend a sixteenth of their money on medical expenses? No, an eighth of it. 5. Do they spend an eighth of their money on the car and bus? No, (only) a sixteenth of it. 6. Do they spend a quarter of their money on entertainment? No, (only) an eighth of it. 7. Do they spend an eighth of their money clothes and miscellaneous? No, (only) a sixteenth of it. 8. Do they put half of their money in savings? No, (only) a

ANSWER KEY 123

sixteenth of it. **B:** 2. three-tenths 3. a tenth 4. tenth 5. A fifth 6. one-twentieth 7. three-twentieths

Unit 74 A: 1. My roommate ate every cookie. 2. My roommate ate those cookies. 3. a little bread 4. that bread/cookie 5. another cookie 6. a few cookies 7. both cookies 8. the other bread/cookie/cookies 9. many cookies 10. my bread/cookie/cookies 11. each cookie 12. the last cookie/cookies **B:** 2. a little, this 3. both, a 4. many, that 5. My, a 6. any, the 7. Some, Their 8. a, The 9. some, Her **C:** a lot of, any, both, no, a lot of

Unit 75 A: 2. the other one 3. a little 4. every one 5. Each 6. another 7. a few 8. little 9. none 10. some 11. another one 12. Each 13. Both 14. few 15. a little **B:** Suggested answers: 2. Phil broke both. 3. Phil has few. 4. Phil has a short one. 5. Phil got many. 6. Phil got none. 7. Phil takes little. 8. Phil reads every one. 9. Phil doesn't want this one.

Unit 76 A: 1. Dick and Janice saw a play in London. 2. The first child and the second one saw an airplane in the sky. 3. We and our neighbors saw an accident in our neighborhood. 4. She saw strange fruit and vegetables in the store. 5. A neighbor saw you and Janice in the park. 6. Dick saw a play and a movie in Paris. 7. The tourists saw plays in London and Paris. 8. She saw birds in the big tree and the little one. 9. We saw water on the floor in the bathroom and the kitchen. 10. John and Jim saw a mouse in the living room. **B:** 2. dimes and nickels 3. paper and pens 4. a carpenter and an electrician 5. the city and the country 6. Mr. Spencer and I 7. a coat and a sweater 8. a magazine and the newspaper 9. Buses and trucks **C:** 2. A phone and a lamp. 3. A blouse and a skirt. 4. The flowers and the tea. 5. A (paper) cup and a (broken) pencil. 6. Pencils and tape.

Unit 77 A: 1. Did Mary tell her friend or Bill? 2. Did Mary tell the librarian or Bill? 3. the librarian or a relative 4. the children or a relative 5. the children or the neighbors 6. Mrs. Sash or Mr. Sash 7. the secretary or her boss 8. you or your brother 9. your brother or her brother 10. the first man or the second one **B:** 2. or (a) magazine 3. or pants 4. or (a) girl's name 5. or a hot one 6. or furniture 7. or the bank 8. or jelly 9. or the passenger 10. or lawyers **C:** 2. Is the lady using knives or scissors? She's using a scissors. 3. Is she holding a vase or a lamp? She's holding a vase. 4. Is she wearing a skirt or pants? She's wearing a skirt. 5. Is it day or night? It's day. 6. Is that a picture of a house or a barn on the wall? It's (a picture of) a barn.

Unit 78 A: 1. Your shoes are in the closet. 2. A mouse is in the closet. 3. A mouse is a quiet animal. 4. That cat is a quiet animal. 5. That cat is lazy. 6. I am lazy. 7. I am on the phone. 8. She is on the phone. 9. She is the new manager. 10. She is forty years old. 11. The houses are forty years old. 12. The houses are near the road. **B:** 2. b; j, m, n, o; u 3. c; k, o, p; q 4. e; k, p; x, q 5. c, h; i, l, m, n, o; q, r, t, u, v, w 6. g; j, m, o; q, r, s, u, v, w 7. d; l; q, w 8. f, c; i, l, m, n, o; q, r, t, u, w, x NOTE: k requires *was* or *were*; p requires *will be*; all others may be any tense. **C:** Suggested answers: 1. Is the ball big? Yes, it is. 2. Is the child on a tricycle? Yes he is. 3. Is the lady angry? No, she isn't. 4. Is her dress wet? Yes, it is. 5. Is the glass on the bench? No, it isn't. 6. Are the flowers by the house? Yes, they are. 7. Are the lady's shoes on? No, they aren't.

Unit 79 A: 1. Does it turn red? No, it doesn't. It turns brown. 2. Does it turn strong? No, it doesn't. It turns weak. 3. Does it taste strong? 4. Does it taste awful? 5. Does it feel awful? 6. Does it feel terrible? 7. Does it sound terrible? 8. Does it sound old? 9. Does it seem old? 10. Does it taste like coffee? 11. Does it taste like coffee? 12. Does it taste like fish? **B:** 2. e,m (That noise sounded like a cow. It didn't sound like a pig.) 3. a,k (The air feels cold. It doesn't feel hot.) 4. d,p 5. f,n 6. c,j 7. h,o 8. b,i. **C:** Suggested answers: 1. seem busy 2. look excited 3. look dirty 4. smells fresh 5. look expensive 6. feels soft 7. sound noisy

Unit 80 A: 1. Does that bottle hold a gallon? No, it doesn't. It holds two quarts. 2. Does a fish have feet? No, it doesn't. It has fins. 3. Does . . . No, he doesn't. He draws maps. 4. No, he didn't. He used a pen. 5. No, he didn't. He drank milk. 6. No, she didn't. She wrote a poem. 7. No, they didn't. They lost the second game. 8. No, it won't. It'll bring blankets. 9. No, she won't. She'll visit Scotland. 10. No, he won't. He'll fight Sal. 11. No, I won't. I'll call the Byrite Company. **B:** 1. touched one player's arm. 2. doesn't burn his old newspapers. 3. killed many rats in the city. 4. moved the sofa to the other side. 5. don't understand English well. 6. will spend about $50 at the restaurant. 7. don't allow dogs inside. **C:** Suggested answers: 2. She crossed the street. Then she entered the store. 3. She opened the can of soda pop. Then she drank it. 4. He'll sell his car. Then he'll buy a motorcycle.

Unit 81 A: 1. Does a dog moo? No, it doesn't. It barks. 2. Does a penguin fly? No, it doesn't. It swims. 3. No, it doesn't. It rises in the east. 4. No, he didn't. He called. 5. No, she didn't. She failed. 6. No, he didn't. He drove. 7. No, they didn't. They stayed inside. 8. No, she won't. She'll dance. 9. No, he won't. He'll forget. 10. No, they won't. They'll win. 11. No, they won't. They'll stay late. **B:** 1. Florence speaks loudly. 2. My brother didn't understand. 3. Some people learn fast. 4. The Greens are leaving now. 5. They are going to vote on Tuesday. 6. Al will drive to the airport. 7. The Giants don't play in St. Louis. **C:** 2. He worked in the yard. He didn't play. 3. The rabbit ran fast. It escaped. 4. The traffic signal changed. The traffic stopped.

Unit 82 A: 1. Mrs. Jones bought her husband a new shirt. 2. Mr. Brown is paying Mr. Green a hundred dollars. 3. . . . showing a customer the spring coats. 4. . . . lend people money. 5. . . . gives students advice. 6. . . . read my son a story. 7. . . . teaching Pedro English. 8. . . . tell us the answer. 9. . . . sending him messages. 10. . . . get Donna a bracelet. 11. . . . make Dave a bowl of soup. **B:** Suggested answers: 1. Christine got her father a book for Christmas. 2. . . . got her sister a game. 3. . . . got her brother a soccer ball. 4. . . . got her boyfriend Jerry a record. 5. . . . got her grandmother a sweater. **C:** 1. sold them 600 boxes last year. 2. didn't find us a seat in that row. 3. isn't giving him a gift on his birthday. 4. asked her father a hard question yesterday. 5. was making his mother a birthday card last night. 6. gave some people tickets on Grand Avenue. 7. is baking her family a pie in the kitchen.

Unit 83 A: 2. found them for me 3.

bought it for him 4. sent them to us 5. taught it to them 6. gave them to her 7. made it for him 8. brought it to her 9. told it to me 10. leave them for them 11. sold them to us 12. will lend them to you **B:** 1. No, Fred owed it to her. 2. No, Emily gave them to me. 3. No, Walter left it for me. 4. No, I make them for them. 5. No, his sister is reading it to him. 6. No, his grandmother was writing one to him. 7. No, Tony and Marie were getting one for her. 8. No, Mr. Cook will show the house to them. 9. No, Carol is going to bring it to you. **C:** Suggested answers: 2. That boy is lending his coat to the girl. 3. That girl is buying a wallet for a man. 4. That woman is telling a story to her friend.

Unit 84 A: 2. doesn't 3. didn't 4. isn't 5. doesn't 6. don't 7. weren't 8. doesn't 9. isn't 10. aren't 11. didn't 12. wasn't **B:** Suggested answers: 1. A penguin is a bird. It isn't a fish. 2. Clara Norris writes books. She doesn't write music. 3. Rabbits eat vegetables. They don't eat meat. 4. My car's a Ford. It isn't a Volkswagen. 5. I drive a Ford. I don't drive a Volkswagen. 6. Those books are dictionaries. They aren't textbooks. 7. Jenny reads magazines. She doesn't read the newspaper. 8. Jerry wears a heavy sweater. He doesn't wear a coat. 9. I eat fruit. I don't eat candy. 10. Mr. Ortega is a Peruvian. He isn't a Mexican. 11. He sells insurance. He doesn't sell houses. **C:** 2. Is he a pilot? Yes, he is. 3. Does that man have his gate pass? No, he doesn't. 4. Is that man getting wet? Yes, he is.

Unit 85 A: 1. There were candles on the cake. 2. There was a big candle on the cake. 3. There was a big candle in the box. 4. There's a big candle in the box. 5. There will be a big candle in the box. 6. There will be a big candle on the table. 7. There will be gifts on the table. 8. There will be gifts for the children. 9. There are going to be gifts for the children. 10. There's going to be a party for the children. 11. There's going to be a party on your birthday. 12. There's going to be a surprise on your birthday. **B:** 2. some Japanese//I know, but there weren't any Greeks at the party. 3. stars//I know, but there aren't any letters on the American flag. 4. a furniture sale//I know, but there won't be a book sale in February. 5. an English test//I know, but there isn't going to be a science test tomorrow. 6. clowns//I know, but there aren't any skaters at the circus. 7. on the vegetables//I know, but there wasn't a lot of/much salt on the meat. 8. in the bedroom//I know, but there wasn't a light on in the living room. 9. for the reporters//I know, but there aren't any seats for the photographers. 10. next year//I know, but there won't be an election (one) this year. 11. on the shelf//I know, but there isn't a soup bowl (one) on the counter. 12. on this seat//I know, but there isn't room for two people on that seat. **C:** 1. There's a broken vase on the floor. 2. There's no knife in the room. 3. There are some flowers on the rug. 4. There aren't any photographers there. 5. There was a fight in the room.

Unit 86 A: 1. Are there bus stops in Rockville? 2. Is there a sports field in Rockville? 3. Was there a sports field in Rockville? 4. Were there fireworks in Rockville? 5. Will there be fireworks in Rockville? 6. Will there be a parade in Rockville? 7. Will there be a parade downtown? 8. Is there going to be a parade downtown? 9. Is there going to be a parade in the park? 10. Are there going to be speeches in the park? 11. Were there speeches in the park? 12. Was there dancing in the park? **B:** 1. there is 2. there aren't 3. there was 4. there weren't 5. there will (be) 6. there won't (be) 7. there are 8. there won't (be) 9. there is 10. there wasn't 11. there are **C:** Suggested answers: 1. Is there going to be a circus parade? No, there isn't. 2. Will there be elephants in the circus? Yes, there will (be). 3. Are there going to be fireworks? Yes, there are. 4. Are there clowns in this circus? Yes, there are. 5. Will there be leopards in the circus? No, there won't (be).

Unit 87 A: 1. Who is rolling on the floor? 2. What is rolling on the floor? 3. What fell 4. What was lying 5. Who was lying 6. Who writes 7. Who didn't sit 8. Who wasn't sitting 9. Who wants to sleep 10. Who is going to sit 11. Who made these marks 12. What made these marks **B:** 1. Who told the whole story? My father did. 2. Who works in a restaurant? A waiter does. 3. Who was on the porch? Betty was. 4. What was ruining the plastic roof? The sun was. 5. What are little and gray? Mice are. 6. What has stripes? Tigers do. 7. Who will fix the lights? The electrician will. 8. Who owns that green car? Earl does. 9. What cuts paper? A scissors does. 10. What's playing at the Palace? *War and Peace* is. 11. Who goes to medical school? Doctors do. **C:** 2. What's burning? A shoe is. Who's holding his nose? That boy is. 3. What broke? A vase did. Who's picking up the pieces? That woman is. 4. Who wrote that letter? Peter did. Who's reading the letter? That woman is.

Unit 88 A: 1. What did you put in the closet? 2. Who did she meet on the bus? 3. What does she make in her free time? 4. What do they keep in that room? 5. Who are they sending to the conference? 6. What is he reading in the newspaper? 7. What is she making for the picnic? 8. Who will you ask about it? 9. Who is he going to help on Saturday? 10. Who was Bonnie telling about her trip? 11. What were they fighting about? 12. Who are you looking for? 13. Who did Pat play chess with? 14. What is she going to change into? **B:** 1. What did Helen bake? She baked bread. 2. What do you like? I like strawberry ice cream. 3. What's Mr. Anh studying? He's studying French. 4. Who(m) is Stan going to invite? He's going to invite Stella. 5. What did Phil lose? He lost his toothbrush. 6. What are you ordering? I'm ordering fish. 7. Who(m) does Mary look like? She looks like her father. 8. What will Hank paint? He'll paint the walls. 9. What does Nicole want to sit on? She wants to sit on the rug. 10. Who(m) did Nicole thank? She thanked Mrs. Benson. 11. What are those people waiting for? They're waiting for the number 5 bus. **C:** Suggested answers: What's the girl wearing? What's she eating? What's under the bed? Who's in that picture? What does she keep in the closet? What did she take out of the box? What was she eating? Who did she receive the necklace from? Where did she go last summer?

Unit 89 A: 1. Which camera are they using? 2. Which camera were they using? 3. was she using? 4. will she get? 5. will you get? 6. do you like? 7. are you keeping? 8. is Mr. Kidd keeping? 9. did Mr. Kidd break? 10. is Mr. Kidd going to take? 11. are the Turners going to take? 12. do the Turners want to sell? **B:** 1. Which ones did she lock? Rooms 506 and 508. 2. Which one is she painting? Judy's bedroom. 3. Which one did you break? 4. Which ones did he read? 5. Which ones will you learn? 6. Which one was she climbing through? 7. Which one does he want to join? 8. Which ones are they going to change? 9. Which ones do you list? 10. Which one will you take? 11. Which ones does he visit? **C:** Suggested answers: Which buses go to Acorn Plaza? Buses number 6 and 8. Which gate does the Oakview bus stop at? Gate C.

Unit 90 A: 2. e 3. c 4. b 5. h 6. a 7. g 8. f **B:** 1. Whose did you use? 2. Whose do you swim in? 3. Whose does he want? 4. Whose is she going to take? 5. Whose was he wearing? 6. Whose did he fill? 7. Whose did she drink from? 8. Whose will she stay at? 9. Whose is he carrying? 10. Whose are you fixing? **C:** 2. Whose history book is that? It's Roger's. 3. Whose girlfriend is that? It's Roger's. 4. Whose glasses are those? They're Roger's. 5. Whose calculator is that? It's Fred's. 6. Whose water glass is that? It's Roger's. 7. Whose camera is that? It's Roger's. 8. Whose radio is on the table? It's Fred's. 9. Whose coat is that? It's Roger's. 10. Whose letters are on the bed? They're Roger's. 11. Whose cookies are they? They're Fred's.

Unit 91 A: 1. He will cook eggs. Where will he cook them? In the kitchen. 2. He cooked the eggs. Where did he cook them? In the kitchen. 3. He is going to cook eggs. Where is he going to cook them? 4. They are going to cook eggs. Where are they going to cook them? 5. They cook eggs. Where do they cook them? 6. They were cooking eggs. Where were they cooking them? 7. They are cooking eggs. Where are they cooking them? 8. I am cooking eggs. Where are you cooking them? 9. I was cooking eggs. Where were you cooking them? 10. I cooked eggs. Where did you cook them? 11. I want to cook eggs. Where do you want to cook them? 12. She wants to cook eggs. Where does she want to cook them? **B:** 1. Where was Miss Hinders? In Bangkok. 2. Where do tigers live? In Southeast Asia. 3. Where did Don park? On the street. 4. Where's the White House? In Washington. 5. Where are toys? On the seventh floor. 6. Where will the boat show be? In Houston. 7. Where was John living? On Elm Street. 8. Where were their kids playing? In the neighbor's. 9. Where's she wearing it? On her right side. 10. Where's Mr. Lachowicz going to teach? In Detroit. 11. Where are the German tourists going? To the southwestern states. **C:** 1. Where do the children play cards? In the dining room. 2. Where do they eat dinner? In the kitchen/dining room. 3. Where do the children do their homework? In the dining room. 4. Where do they take baths? In the bathroom. 5. Where do they watch TV? In the living room. 6. Where do they sleep? In the bedroom. 7. Where do they keep the bird? In the bedroom. 8. Where does Mrs. Crooks write letters? In the living room. 9. Where do they have the phone? In the hall.

Unit 92 A: 1. She's going to read the newspaper. When's she going to read it? In the morning. 2. She'll read the newspaper. When will she read it? In the morning. 3. They'll read, When will they read 4. They read, When do they read 5. They're going to read, When are they going to read 6. I'm going to read, When are you going to read 7. I read, When do you read 8. I'll read, When will you read 9. I read, When did you read 10. We read, When did you read 11. We'll read, When will you read 12. We're going to read, When are you going to read **B:** 1. When will it clear up? This afternoon. 2. When was he there/at the dentist's? On Tuesday. 3. When did she cut it? 4. When were you feeling bad? 5. When were they leaving? 6. When do you get it? 7. When will it be there/in the stores? 8. When did they get angry? 9. When does she change them? 10. When is it going to go up? 11. When does the driver want to take it? **C:** Suggested answers: 1. When will Mr. F. call his wife? At 3:30 in the afternoon. 2. When did Mr. F. interview Miss Adams? At 11:00. 3. When will Mr. F. go for lunch? At 12:30. 4. When will Mr. F. call Atlanta? 5. When will Mr. F. call Sal?

Unit 93 A: 1. How many toys were in the box? 2. How much rice was in the box? 3. How many mice were 4. How much money was 5. How many coins were 6. How many coins will go 7. How many bottles will go 8. How much wood will go 9. How much wood did you put 10. How many socks did you put 11. How much food did you put 12. How much food is **B:** 1. How many is she learning? A dozen. 2. How many do you see? Nine or ten. 3. How much did he buy? 4. How many will they need? 5. How many are you going to buy? 6. How much went bad? 7. How many didn't she find? 8. How many drank it? 9. How much wasn't good? 10. How many were lying there/on the sofa? 11. How many were down? **C:** Suggested answers: How much gas is on the road? A lot. How many policemen are at the accident? Three. How many people are watching? One. How much broken glass is there around? A little. How many people are still in the cars? One.

Unit 94 A: 2. Who, Harold did. 3. What, In a tent. 4. Whose, Harold's. 5. How much, 35 pounds. 6. When, On July eleventh. 7. Which, His left one. 8. When, The next day. 9. How long, Eight days. **B:** Suggested answers: What's the name of this street? It's Broad Street. Where is it? It's in Rockdale. Where's the dog? On the sidewalk. Who's crossing the street? A young couple. How many cars do you see? Only one. What's the cab driver doing? He's waiting for a light. **C:** Suggested answers: 1. Which one did he bring? His math book. 2. Whose will we go in? Mr. Cook's. 3. How much did he drink? One glass. 4. Which one did you lose? The left one. 5. Who did you give it to? The Johnsons. 6. When are we going to have it? Tomorrow. 7. Which day did it rain? Tuesday. 8. How many did you look at? Hundreds of them.

Unit 95 A: 1. They aren't cold, are they? 2. They're cold, aren't they? 3. They were cold, weren't they? 4. It was cold, wasn't it? 5. It wasn't cold, was it? 6. It isn't cold, is it? 7. It's cold, isn't it? 8. It'll be cold, won't it? 9. He'll be cold, won't he? 10. He won't be cold, will he? 11. You won't be cold, will you? 12. I won't be cold, will I? **B:** 1. The airplane isn't ready, is it? No, it isn't. 2. The car is a taxi, isn't it? Yes, it is. 3. are you? No, I'm not. 4. aren't they? Yes, they are. 5. won't he? Yes, he will. 6. was it? No, it wasn't. 7. wasn't it? Yes, it was. 8. weren't they? Yes, they were. 9. were they? No, they weren't. 10. will he/she? No, he/she won't. 11. aren't they? Yes, they are. 12. isn't it? Yes, it is. 13. are they? No, they aren't. 14. aren't I? Yes, you are. **C:** Suggested answers: 1. Her shoes are wet, aren't they? Yes, they are. 2. Her father isn't happy, is he? No, he isn't. 3. The record was under her jacket, wasn't it? Yes, it was. 4. Her hair isn't dry, is it? No, it isn't.

Unit 96 A: 1. The dogs aren't riding in the car, are they? 2. The dogs aren't sleeping in the car, are they? 3. Clara isn't sleeping in the car, is she? 4. Clara's reading in the car, isn't she? 5. Clara and you are reading in the car, aren't you? 6. Clara and you aren't fighting, are you? 7. Clara and you were singing, weren't you? 8. The driver was singing, wasn't he/she? 9. The driver isn't singing, is he/she? 10. The driver's laughing, isn't he/she? 11. The children are laughing, aren't they? 12. The children are telling jokes, aren't they? **B:** 1. Jeff was sitting on the sofa, wasn't he? Yes, he was. 2. Jeff was feeling tired, wasn't he? Yes, he was. 3. Jeff wasn't reading, was he? No, he wasn't. 4. Jeff was sleeping, wasn't he? Yes, he was. 5. His mother was cooking supper, wasn't she? Yes, she was. 6. She wasn't washing the dishes, was she? No, she wasn't. 7. Some animals were flying, weren't they? Yes, they were. 8. They weren't making noise, were they? Yes, they were. 9. Jeff was watching them, wasn't he? Yes, he was. 10. The animals were lifting Jeff, weren't they? No, they weren't. 11. One was holding his neck, wasn't it? Yes, it was. 12. His mother was eating, wasn't she? No, she wasn't. **C:** Suggested answers: 2. The dog isn't walking on a rope, is it? No, it isn't. It's jumping over fire. 3. The lady isn't jumping over fire, is she? No, she isn't. She's walking on a rope. 4. The monkeys aren't climbing on the car, are they? No, they aren't. They're riding bicycles.

Unit 97 A: 1. You drink milk, don't you? 2. You didn't drink milk, did you? 3. You don't like milk, do you? 4. She doesn't like milk, does she? 5. She bought milk, didn't she? 6. She didn't have milk, did she? 7. They didn't have milk, did they? 8. They didn't use milk, did they? 9. They don't need milk, do they? 10. They wanted milk, didn't they? 11. The baby wanted milk, didn't he/she? 12. The baby needs milk, doesn't he/she? **B:** 1. Your brother has a watch, doesn't he? Yes, he does. 2. Many people don't like Bill, do they? No, they don't. 3. did she? No, she didn't. 4. don't they? Yes, they do. 5. doesn't he? Yes, he does. 6. didn't they? Yes, they did. 7. didn't he? Yes, he did. 8. did they? No, they didn't. 9. does it? No, it doesn't. 10. didn't you? Yes, I did. 11. doesn't he? Yes, he does. 12. did you? No, I didn't. 13. didn't she? Yes, she did. 14. doesn't it? Yes, it does. **C:** 1. Danny doesn't draw well, does he? Yes, he does. 2. He didn't win any ribbons, did he? Yes, he did. 3. He doesn't play soccer, does he? Yes, he does. 4. He listens to pop music, doesn't he? Yes, he does.

Unit 98 A: 1. There are eggs in the cake, aren't there? Yes, there are. 2. There are nuts in the cake, aren't there? No, there aren't. 3. There's butter . . . isn't there? Yes, there is. 4. There are raisins . . . aren't there? No, there aren't. 5. There's chocolate . . . isn't there? Yes, there is. 6. There's salt . . . isn't there? No, there isn't. 7. There's milk . . . isn't there? Yes, there is. 8. There are berries . . . aren't there? No, there aren't. 9. There's brown sugar . . . isn't there? No, there isn't. **B:** 2. are there? 3. won't there? 4. aren't there? 5. are there? 6. wasn't there? 7. were there? 8. There wasn't 9. weren't there? 10. There's 11. There was 12. won't there? **C:** Suggested answers: 1. There weren't any tall buildings in 1946, were there? No, there weren't. 2. There was no post office in 1946, was there? Yes, there was. 3. There weren't many people on the streets in 1946, were there? No, there weren't. 4. There will be a new bank building soon, won't there? Yes, there will.

Unit 99 A: 1. does he? 2. didn't he? 3. wasn't he? 4. don't they? 5. did she? 6. isn't it? 7. aren't they? 8. did you? 9. aren't they? 10. was it? 11. will he? 12. are there? 13. did you? 14. were they? 15. didn't they? 16. isn't there? 17. were they? 18. didn't it? 19. won't we? 20. isn't he? 21. is she? **B:** 1. One person is buying toothpaste, isn't he? Yes, he is. 2. That man got a lamp, didn't he? Yes, he did. 3. Those children don't like candy, do they? Yes, they do. 4. The lady's going to read a magazine, isn't she? Yes, she is. 5. The cashier's giving the man change, isn't she? Yes, she is. 6. There are ten people in line, aren't there? No, there aren't.

Unit 100 A: 1. Aren't the Hochs from Ireland? No, they aren't. 2. Isn't Marie from Ireland? No, she isn't. 3. Isn't Marie tall? Yes, she is. 4. Isn't Charles tall? No, he isn't. 5. Isn't the carpenter tall? Yes, he is. 6. Isn't the carpenter on the roof? No, he isn't. 7. Aren't the nails on the roof? No, they aren't. 8. Aren't the nails in your pocket? Yes, they are. 9. Isn't the key in your pocket? Yes, it is. 10. Isn't the key new? No, it isn't. 11 Aren't those shoes new? Yes, they are. 12. Aren't those (shoes) your good shoes? Yes, they are. **B:** 1. Wasn't that meat $1.29 (a pound)? No, it wasn't. It was $2.19. 2. Weren't your socks in the bottom drawer? No, they weren't. They were in the top drawer. 3. Wasn't that woman Italian? No, she wasn't. She was Indian. 4. Wasn't Mrs. Frazer in Room 423? No, she wasn't. She was in Room 424. 5. Weren't the cups empty? No, they weren't. They were full. 6. Weren't the vegetables peas? No, they weren't. They were carrots. 7. Weren't the berries sweet? No, they weren't. They were sour. **C:** 1. Oh, isn't it rising? 2. Oh, isn't she studying? 3. Oh, isn't he painting the kitchen? 4. Oh, aren't they staying here? 5. Oh, aren't they singing tomorrow night? 6. Oh, wasn't he swimming? 7. Oh, wasn't she teaching English? 8. Oh, weren't they baking in the oven? 9. Oh, weren't they putting up a traffic light?

Unit 101 A: 1. Doesn't Mr. Clark speak German? 2. Don't those people speak German? 3. Don't those people come from Germany? 4. Doesn't Klaus come from Germany? 5. Doesn't Klaus want a sandwich? 6. Doesn't Klaus know John's address? 7. Doesn't Klaus live on Maple Street? 8. Don't the Jacksons live on Maple Street? 9. Don't the Jackson's have two cars? 10. Doesn't Marcia have two cars? 11. Doesn't Marcia play the guitar? 12. Don't your brothers play the guitar? **B:** 1. Doesn't Henry paint pictures? No, he paints houses. 2. Don't Tigers live in Africa? No, they live in Asia. 3. Doesn't Mrs. Thorpe work in a factory? No, she works in an office. 4. Doesn't Clara buy her clothes? No she makes them (herself). 5. Didn't the children want candy? No they wanted ice cream (cones). 6. Doesn't the bank open at 9 o'clock? No, it opens at 10 o'clock. 7. Didn't the Marinos go to the beach? No, they went to the mountains. **C:** 1. Oh, don't you like pie? 2. Oh, doesn't it have ink in it? 3. don't they 4. didn't they 5. didn't they 6. didn't she 7. didn't she 8. doesn't he 9. doesn't it

Unit 102 A: 1. at 2. in 3. in 4. on 5. in 6. at, in 7. on 8. in 9. at 10. on 11. in. 12. in **B:** 1. away from, X, to, into 2. off of, out of, into, in 3. on, in, at, out of, in, on 4. at/in, on, out of, to/into, on, on.

Unit 103 A: 1. They're moving today. 2. They moved yesterday. 3. will move 4. will move 5. are moving/will move/moved 6. moved 7. will move/are moving 8. moved 9. are moving/will move/moved 10. will move 11. moved 12. will move. **B:** Suggested answers: 1. No, he won't. He'll come at 3:00 o'clock. 2. No, they won't. They'll start in March. 3. No, they won't. They'll start in 1988. 4. No, she didn't. She called on his birthday. 5. No, she didn't. She called at midnight. 6. No, I didn't. I bought it in 1975. 7. No, I didn't. I bought it in January. 8. No, it doesn't. It leaves at 10:00. 9. No, he doesn't. He needs it on the first of the month. 10. No, we don't. We need it on Tuesday. 11. No, we don't. We need it on the first of the month. **C:** 1. Are you getting up at 6:00 (tomorrow morning)? No, I'm getting up at 5:30. 2. Will they be away in August? No, they'll be away in July. Are they going to leave on July 1? Yes, they're going to leave on July 1. 3. Was Edison born in 1863? No, he was born in 1847. Did Lindbergh die in 1947? No, he died in 1974.

Unit 104 A: 1. She enjoyed herself downtown the other day. 2. She enjoyed herself in Little Rock the other day. 3. in Little Rock last week. 4. at the farm last week. 5. at the farm this summer. 6. on the beach in the summer. 7. on the beach all afternoon. 8. in the park all afternoon. 9. in the park at lunchtime. 10. on the playground at lunchtime. 11. on the playground for an hour. 12. away from the office for an hour. **B:** 1. in Cairo at 1:30. 2. in the garage tomorrow. 3. in the hospital last year. 4. downstairs in the winter. 5. in the post office on April 13. 6. to Yellowstone a few days from now. 7. in Louisiana for three years. 8. in the refrigerator after breakfast. 9. out of his pocket immediately. 10. at the beach this summer. 11. by the front door before dark. 12. in school Friday night. 13. this evening. 14. in their back yard a few days ago. **C:** Suggested answers: 1. The bus leaves for Omaha at 12:10. The Rochester bus gets here at 9:30. 2. There will be a soccer game at Independence on Saturday. He'll sit in Section 4 on October 15. 3. He called Little Rock on December 4. He spoke to a friend in Minnesota for eight minutes on December 31.

Unit 105 A: 1. She seldom looks at Dan's picture. 2. always looks 3. didn't always look 4. didn't usually look 5. was usually looking 6. was sometimes looking 7. was never looking 8. never looked 9. seldom looked 10. often looked 11. wasn't often looking 12. wasn't always looking **B:** 1. Our bank account is always low. 2. were usually 3. was never 4. is often waiting 5. is sometimes going to miss 6. I'm never going to stay 7. They always ask 8. sometimes parks 9. always leaves 10. seldom locked 11. often flew 12. will sometimes take 13. usually change **C:** Suggested answers: Did Kim get A on a test last year? Yes, she always did. Did Kim get B on a test last year? No, she never did. Did Costas get A on a test last year? Yes, he often did. Did Costas get B on a test last year? Yes, he sometimes did.

Unit 106 A: 2. and, has 3. and, are playing 4. and, reads 5. and, ate 6. and, are going to 7. and, took off 8. and, ordered 9. and, sells 10. and, comes from 11. and, was cooking 12. and, left, home **B:** 1. The mailman came and brought us two letters and a magazine. 2. Esther was sitting at the table and was eating cake. 3. Buses stop at that corner and pick up passengers. 4. Mr. Dunbar bought balloons and gave them to the kids. 5. Miss Hoff was on the beach all day and got a sunburn. 6. Mrs. Boyd will paint the room and wash out the brushes. 7. Miss Cummings cleaned the blackboard for the teacher and sat down. 8. Donald is a doctor and works at football games. 9. They parked the car and locked it for the night. 10. Ruth bought apples and made an apple pie. 11. We have to catch the dog and give it a bath. **C:** Suggested answers: The Powells grow flowers, and the Troutens grow vegetables. The Troutens live in a brick house, and the Powells live in a wooden one. The Troutens have a small car, and the Powells have a big one.

Unit 107 A: 1. but Clara used a knife. 2. but Allen is afraid of dark places. 3. but Ben wants to play basketball. 4. but they don't have pictures. 5. but he doesn't feel well. 6. but Bakersfield is in the valley. **B:** 1. she can't walk. 2. I'm not going to wash it. 3. Mark doesn't like California. 4. she drives to the library. 5. he didn't put it back under the desk. 6. Florence cleaned it up. 7. Frank has his skates. 8. he didn't earn much money. **C:** 2. but she didn't have any 24-cent stamps. 3. but she's not good in art. 4. but it isn't working. 5. but I watched it on TV. 6. but he got hurt.

Unit 108 A: 1. but Tom is 2. but my boots aren't 3. but the movie did 4. but her watch didn't 5. but the children weren't 6. but I'm not 7. but Barbara was 8. but dark shirts don't 9. but penguins can't 10. but ours didn't 11. but the 5:30 bus won't 12. but that one will 13. but the drugstore does **B:** 1. No. The Ford needs it, but not the Volkswagen. 2. No. Tulips come out then/in April, but not roses. 3. No. Mrs. Stanhope is over forty years old, but not Mrs. Stoll. 4. No. Anna Mae will be there/at the meeting, but not Ruth. 5. No. She sews dresses, but not shirts. 6. No. It has a lion, but not a tiger. 7. No. She is wearing regular blue jeans, but not designer jeans. 8. No. She wants to plant vegetables, but not flowers. 9. No. I cut my left hand, but not my right one. 10. No. It's going to be cloudy, but it isn't going to rain. 11. No. He/She gave me vitamin C, but not vitamin E. 12. No. The Moseleys have two daughters, but the Boons don't. 13. No. It was in the morning and evening, but not in the afternoon. **C:** Suggested answers: Jean is from France, but Jiro isn't. Jean has a surfboard but Jiro doesn't. Jiro plays baseball, but Jean doesn't. Jean doesn't wear eyeglasses, but Jiro does.

Unit 109 A: 2. and 3. but 4. but 5. and

6. and 7. but 8. and 9. and 10. but **B:** 2. but (he) b 3. and g 4. and (he) h 5. but c 6. but (he) a 7. and (he) e 8. and (I) f **C:** Suggested answers: 2. and found a handkerchief 3. and it almost covered the benches 4. but the phone rang 5. but it wasn't in the book 6. and the bread in the cabinet

Unit 110 A: 1. g 2. e 3. c 4. f 5. h 6. d 7. a 8. b **B:** 1. or borrow it 2. or buy them 3. or call/drive there 4. or drive/walk (there) 5. or forget them 6. or keep them 7. or resting/eating/walking/driving 8. or laughing 9. or reading/eating/walking 10. or reading/eating/walking/resting 11. or call him

C: Suggested answers: 2. Are you going to ski or skate? 3. Is the boy going to play ball or help his father? 4. Is she going to phone her friend or write him/her a letter?

APPENDIX A — Noun Modifiers and Substitutes

	With Plural Count Nouns		With Mass Nouns		With Singular Count Nouns	
Indefinites (Quantifiers & Other)	[no modifier]	SOME, ANY	[no modifier]	SOME, ANY	a, an	ONE
	some	SOME	some	SOME	———	———
	any	ANY	any	ANY	———	———
	a few	A FEW	a little	A LITTLE	———	———
	a lot of	A LOT	a lot of	A LOT	———	———
	many	MANY	much	MUCH	———	———
	few	FEW	little	LITTLE	———	———
	no	NONE	no	NONE	———	———
	all	ALL	all	ALL	every	EVERY ONE
	both	BOTH	———	———	each	EACH (ONE)
	two, etc.	TWO, etc.	———	———	one	ONE
	other	OTHER (ONE)S	other	OTHER	another	ANOTHER (ONE)
Definites	the	THEY, WE, YOU THEM, US, YOU THEM-, OUR-, YOURSELVES	the	IT IT ITSELF	the	I, YOU, HE, SHE, IT ME, YOU, HIM, HER, IT MY-, YOUR-, HIM-, HER-, ITSELF
	my, our, his, her, its, your, their	MINE, OURS, HIS, HERS, YOURS, THEIRS	my, etc.	MINE, etc.	my, etc.	MINE, etc.
	these	THESE	this	THIS	this	THIS (ONE)
	those	THOSE	that	THAT	that	THAT (ONE)
	the first, etc.	THE FIRST (ONES), etc.	———	———	the first, etc.	THE FIRST (ONE), etc.
	the other	THE OTHER (ONE)S	the other	THE OTHER	the other	THE OTHER (ONE)

NOTE: Articles and other modifiers are in lower case letters; personal pronouns and other substitutes are in upper case.

APPENDIX B — Past Tense of Irregular Verbs

begin/began	do/did	forget/forgot	hurt/hurt	put/put	shut/shut	tell/told
break/broke	draw/drew	get/got	know/knew	read/read	sing/sang	think/thought
bring/brought	drink/drank	give/gave	leave/left	ride/rode	sit/sat	understand/understood
build/built	drive/drove	go/went	lend/lent	ring/rang	sleep/slept	wake/woke
buy/bought	eat/ate	grow/grew	lie/lay	run/ran	speak/spoke	wear/wore
catch/caught	fall/fell	have/had	lose/lost	say/said	spend/spent	win/won
come/came	feel/felt	hear/heard	make/made	see/saw	stand/stood	write/wrote
cost/cost	find/found	hit/hit	mean/meant	sell/sold	take/took	
cut/cut	fly/flew	hold/held	meet/met	send/sent	teach/taught	

	No Vowel Change	Vowel Change
No Suffix	cost, cut, hit, hurt, put, shut	begin, break, come, draw, drink, drive, eat, fall, find, fly, forget, get, give, grow, hold, know, lie, meet, read, ride, ring, run, see, sing, sit, speak, stand, take, understand, wake, wear, win, write
-t Suffix	build, lend send, spend	bring, buy, catch, feel, go, leave, lose, mean, sleep, teach, think
-d Suffix	have, make	do, hear, say, sell, tell

APPENDIX C — Types of Sentences

	Subject & Auxiliary (or) Aux. & Subj.		Verb	Indirect Object	Complement or Direct Object	Adverbials
Be	He Is(n't)	is(n't) he	—	—	a child/well/here	(now)
Linking	He Is(n't)	is(n't) he	feeling	—	well	(now)
	He Does(n't)	(doesn't) he	feel	—	well	(now)
Intransitive	He Is(n't)	is(n't) he	writing	—	—	(now)
	He Does(n't)	(doesn't) he	write(s)	—	—	(often)
Transitive	He Is(n't)	is(n't) he	writing	(her)	a letter	(now)
	He Does(n't)	(doesn't) he	write(s)	(her)	a letter	(often)
There	There Is(n't)	isn't there	—	—	an egg	(there now)